The Sound of His Voice

Everyday Principles for Listening to God

Carol Marquardt

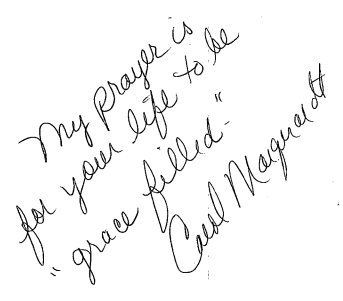

Mantle Publishing
Clearwater, Florida

Published by Mantle Publishing
P.O. Box 2931
Clearwater, Florida 33757-2931

ISBN: 0-9700580-3-9

Cover photo by Mark Marquardt.
Cover art, design and book layout by Jeff Signorini,
jsGrafx Creative Services. Some art by Jeanne Kimbrell.

To my husband, Mark, as holy and loving a man as
I know, for the steady hand, strong shoulder and
gentle support which has come all along the way.

Acknowledgments

I want to acknowledge with great
appreciation: Vicki Krueger, who helped
me get organized and molded my thoughts
and notes into a manuscript; Jeff Signorini,
who provided publishing expertise and
final editing; Fr. Michael Scanlan, TOR,
who provided strong encouragement when
I needed it most. Also, my thanks to Sister
Marjorie Quinn and Ronda Russick for
their background help.

NIHIL OBSTAT:
Bishop Robert N. Lynch, DD
Bishop of the Diocese of St. Petersburg, Florida
Censor Librorum - Fr. David L. Toups, S.T.D.
September 1, 2006

DIOCESE
OF ST. PETERSBURG
Office Of The Bishop

May 23, 2006

Dear Friends in Christ,

OUR FIAT is a program that was developed by a group of active lay people in our diocese out of their desire to explore a deeper relationship with God. It has gained the respect of the pastors in the parishes where the program currently exists. *OUR FIAT* invites Catholics to renew their faith and to develop a deeper prayer life.

I heartily recommend this program for both personal spiritual growth and building bonds of community within parishes. With prayerful best regards, I am

Your friend in Christ Jesus,

Most Reverend Robert N. Lynch
Bishop of St. Petersburg

CONTENTS

Fr. Michael Scanlan's Introduction
to
The Sound of His Voice

I have waited to read a book such as this. I have known Carol Marquardt for the past twenty-five years and have watched her grow in holiness, wisdom and maturity. Yet the importance of this book is that it is written for the ordinary person who is caught up in the ordinary responsibilities and cares of daily life, working and raising a family.

Carol details her experiences which are recounted as ordinary, daily experiences, and yet because of their supernatural nature would be called extraordinary. She hears God in daily life. She receives comfort, guidance and protection through hearing God. She tells the rest of us to open to the Holy Spirit and experience what she experiences.

This is very simple and yet revolutionary for the person who has never encountered God in this way. Carol is not teaching that you will have the same exact experiences that she has. She is teaching that each of us can have a relationship with God through the power of the Holy Spirit that will radically change our lives for the better. We too can say we *hear God*.

Is this just imagination or wishful thinking? The answer is no. This is what is promised us in the Scriptures, and most explicitly in the fourth Gospel.

In John's Gospel, Jesus promises to send us *paracletus* who will teach us all things, remind us of all that He taught us, console and comfort us, be our guide and advocate and the Spirit of Truth to lead us to all truth. This is an overwhelming promise. Our minds cannot embrace all that this could mean.

Here are three key passages:

"If you love me, you will keep my commandments. And I will ask the Father and He will give you another Advocate (paraclete) to be with you always, the Spirit of truth which the world cannot accept because it neither sees nor knows it." (John 14:15-17)

"I have told you this while I am with you. The Advocate (paraclete), the Holy Spirit that the Father will send in my name —He will teach you everything and remind you of all that I told you." (John 14:25-26)

"I have much more to tell you but you cannot bear it now. But when He comes, the Spirit of truth, He will guide you to all truth." (John 16:12-13)

The very word *paracletus* comes from the verb *parakleo*, which can best be understood in this context as *to encourage*, and therefore as a *defense attorney* which will impart courage and advice to those on trial. John is telling us that the world is accusing us and putting us on trial. We are outnumbered by the forces against us but the Holy Spirit—paraclete is given to us so that we might triumph in this life and gain eternal life.

This defense attorney is not just for Church as a body, or for the leaders or a few apostles. John makes it clear that it is for everyone.

The words that Jesus speaks in Matthew's gospel also show that God reveals his word to the little ones:

"I praise you, Father, Lord of heaven and earth, because you have hidden these things from the wise and learned and have revealed them to little children. Yes, Father, for this was your good pleasure." (Matthew 11:25)

The Holy Spirit's assistance is for all of us as long as we are humble enough to know our need and submit to being taught by God.

This gift of the Holy Spirit is so important that Jesus proclaims: "But I tell you the truth, it is better for you that I go. For if I do not go, the Advocate will not come to you." (John 16:7)

Having said all this, how can we be sure that what we experience is in fact God? Furthermore, how can we be sure that our conclusions of what we experience are in fact what God wants and what God wants us to do?

The answer is that we cannot be certain but we can be greatly helped and encouraged by seeking to hear God in a personal way. The Church has always taught that we should seek and reverence God's inspirations in our lives. These inspirations usually lead us to appreciate more the truths of the faith and to commit ourselves more to follow the teaching of the Gospels and the Church.

Recognizing the inspirations of God and growing in prayer so as to receive inspirations in a fuller manner usually happens over a span of time. Indeed, it is growth in the relationship with God that enables us to *hear God* in a better and fuller way.

On occasion, these times of inspiration may include charisms or locutions or visions, but these are exceptions and should not be accepted too easily. On the other hand, we should be very ready to accept inspirations from God when they do not conflict in any way with the clear teaching of the Church.

Some might question why we need these personal inspirations at all. Isn't the Church's teaching through the established channels, including parochial instruction and preaching, enough to inspire and guide us? The history of the Church, particularly the teaching and example of the saints, shows us that God intends to go beyond these to express his personal love, care and guidance for his people.

With these words, I have wanted to address some main concerns that readers might have in the area of *hearing God*. I want to encourage you to read this book. Read it with an open heart and mind. If you do so, you will be better positioned to *hear God* and respond to his will for your life.

Fr. Michael Scanlan, TOR
President, Franciscan University of Steubenville
Author of the book, *What Does God Want?*

AUTHOR'S FOREWORD

Now that we have entered the 21st century, we are as far distant in time from the birth of Jesus as was Abraham before Jesus. Our human awareness and scientific knowledge is vastly different than that of people who lived at the time of Abraham or at the time of Jesus. While God has not changed, our human perspective has. As a result, many sophisticated voices are teaching confusing principles that appear more in keeping with modern society than Jesus' teaching. We who want to follow Jesus need all the help we can get.

My purpose in writing is to suggest to you that we can get the help we need. Through the Holy Spirit we can hear and recognize God's voice in prayer. He knows us each personally and has specific words and inspirations for us individually. Many people miss this beautiful dimension of their faith life simply because they do not expect to hear from the Lord personally and possibly do not know how to recognize his voice. It is my hope that this book will help.

In case you think what I am saying is rather farfetched, let me say that people who know me would tell you I am reasonably intelligent and emotionally stable. Yet I really do believe that the Lord of history speaks directly and personally to me. Additionally, I do not think that I have been singled out for special favors. Rather, this gift of prayer communication is meant for all of us who are trying to follow Jesus.

If you do not already believe this, consider the possibility that God wants to speak directly and personally to you to help you as a disciple of Jesus. He does this through the Holy Spirit, given to each of us to guide us. The Holy Spirit within us communicates with us. In a nutshell, that is the entire point of this book. At the end of each chapter I include a suggested prayer exercise for you to try. Find a few quiet moments and see what happens!

Let me say that I write from a Catholic background and believe in the authenticity of the apostolic teaching of the Catholic Church. But, in addition to following the basic moral and religious teachings of my faith, I believe that God wants an intimate personal relationship with me, based on dialogue in personal prayer. What I am saying in this book relates to that personal relationship and as such is relevant for all Christians. Indeed, intimacy with the Lord likely helps us all to better love and respect one another in our differences, because we come to know the love of God in a more profound way.

Because I am not a theologian, my reflections are based on my own life experiences and those of people to whom I have ministered in prayer over the years. Personal testimony seems to me to be the best way to illustrate principles of prayer communication. It is my hope that, in the stories I tell, you will find encouragement to strengthen your own dialogue with the Lord who seems incredibly willing to walk every step of our life's journey with us.

I came across a Scripture passage just yesterday that I had never read before but which clearly reflects my feelings about this writing. The author of 2 Maccabees said at the close of his narrative: *"If it is well told and to the point, that is what I myself desired; if it is poorly done and mediocre, that was the best I could do."* So be it! May these words be a blessing to you.

Carol Marquardt

Please see the appendix beginning on page 113 for suggestions on using this book as a tool for personal prayer or in a small group setting.

PART ONE:
Believing God Speaks

Chapter One

How God Speaks

L et me start by telling you about my dog Hannah. I got Hannah from a pet store when she was three months old, and she had never heard me speak. As she started living with us, however, she grew familiar with the sound of my voice. Eventually, after dog obedience school, much trial and error, and lots of growing and maturing, she became obedient to my voice. In effect, beyond daily routine, my voice directs Hannah's life. She trusts me and obeys my voice because (dog psychologists tell me) she recognizes me as her dog pack leader. Dogs are instinctively submissive to the leader of their pack.

At one time, I could only take Hannah out into the yard on a leash for fear she would run into the street or run away. But now, because of her training and our relationship, I can protect her with the sound of my voice. She will do what I say. And I know that she will listen and obey out of trust and instinct. Unless, of course, a cat or raccoon comes into view. Then another dog instinct takes over!

In talking about leading us as disciples, Jesus uses a similar analogy: sheep. Jesus refers to himself as a shepherd who lovingly cares for those sheep in his flock. "My sheep recognize my voice and they follow me." Implicit in recognizing his voice, of course, is *hearing* his voice. He speaks in many ways to us: through the Scriptures, through the Church, through teachers and leaders. But He also speaks through the Holy Spirit in our hearts.

I guess Jesus is hopeful that his voice will influence our lives strongly enough to protect us from danger and show us a good path for our journey through this life. He is not present humanly as He was two thousand years ago when He talked about being a good shepherd. But He can still talk to us individually through the Holy Spirit in our hearts. We just need to learn to listen and to recognize his voice.

When Jesus speaks to us on an individual basis He will not add anything new to what has been revealed to all of humanity through salvation history. Rather, his words to us make personal, real, relevant and life-giving those same things that have been revealed throughout history to humanity as a whole. And that helps us to follow him!

The Holy Spirit echoes God's voice in our own hearts and minds. After we are baptized and receive the gift of the Holy Spirit, we can attune ourselves to this Holy Spirit within us and hear God's personal call to friendship and discipleship following Jesus. If you haven't experienced this before now, I encourage you to try listening.

PRAYER EXERCISE ONE

Preparation: Find a quiet corner where you can sit uninterrupted for a period of time. Sit down, gather yourself together and ask the Lord to help you put aside all present worries and thoughts. Quiet yourself. After reading this suggested meditation, close your eyes and try it.

Imagine yourself standing on a beach gazing over the water at the sun. Because the sun is so bright, even in your meditation, you close your eyes. You feel the sun's rays warming you and, though your eyes are closed, you know by the warmth that the sun is still shining over the water.

Now imagine that the sun changes and becomes the person of Jesus. Feel the warm rays continuing to touch you, this time radiating from Jesus. He walks across the water to the beach as you bask in the warmth of the rays. He walks toward you and stops in front of you. He reaches for your hand and says, "I have come to be with you. Would you like for me to stay always near you?"

How do you answer?

"About the fourth watch of the night, He came walking toward them, walking on the sea." (Mark 6:48)

Chapter Two

How We Listen

Attuning ourselves to the Holy Spirit within our hearts is not that easy because we are not necessarily very attentive listeners. Just ask any husbands or wives how well they think their spouses listen to them! Many would surely say, "Not very!" Attentive listening takes effort and focus beyond just hearing!

Here is one typical example of what I mean. One Saturday morning, my husband Mark told me he was going to get a haircut in an hour. He offered to do some errands for me if I needed anything. Then he went into his study to do some work until it was time to leave. After a short while I went into Mark's study and asked him to pick up a remote control I had ordered for our television after the dog had chewed up the original one. I told him the store was located a half-mile south of a certain mall. He lovingly said "sure" and, in a short while, left the house.

A half-hour later, the phone rang. It was Mark, asking, "Where in this mall did you say the TV store is? I don't see it." He had remembered me saying "the mall" but not "one-half-mile south." Trying hard to help me, he was wandering all around the mall, looking for the TV store. Of course, it was not there but rather "one-half-mile south." Mark had missed that part of my directions because I had made my request while he was focused on his project and, consequently, he had only heard a part of my directions. He sincerely wanted to help me but his attention to the project on which he was working had distracted him from completely focusing on my request.

We are tempted to listen to God in a similar manner. We have interests and projects of our own which distract us from God's voice and take our focus away from him. We truly want to please him. We are willing to do what He wants. We just simply are not always attentive to what He is saying. We go about our daily routine not really expecting to hear from God. We can miss his voice even when He is truly speaking to us.

There is a train track about a block from our house. Trains pass by several times a day, whistling at a nearby crossing. But do you know that I only notice that whistle about once a year? I don't notice because I have gotten used to it and am not attentive to it.

In order to be receptive to all that the Lord would say to us through the Holy Spirit, we need to bring what I call *the three S's* into our daily lives. These are three time and tradition tested disciplines that help to overcome the human frailty of inattentiveness. The three S's are: stillness, silence and solitude.

STILLNESS

I have never forgotten this simple story I heard years ago. A husband and wife were driving to a fancy restaurant to celebrate their anniversary. The wife said to her husband, "Honey, do you remember the days when we were dating, and I would sit right next to you in the driver's seat? Now here I am, hugging the window." Her husband glanced across the seat and said simply, "I haven't moved."

We have this tendency to slide away from the embrace of God by becoming overly absorbed in busy activities of our own private world. We can find ourselves over by the window. How can we move across the space in the middle of the seat and stay within God's reach so He can put his arm around us? We can do it by slowing down, by becoming still. Temporarily we put aside the busyness that consumes our attention in order to really hear what the Holy Spirit is saying to us.

SILENCE

Stepping aside from our activities isn't always enough to listen attentively. We must then stop talking. We learn to be good talkers because we want to get our needs expressed, to have our ideas heard, to verbally defend ourselves and to negotiate our way with others; in short, to look out for our interests. Sometimes, unfortunately, this sort of talking also describes our relationship with God in prayer. In order to hear him, we need to stop negotiating, to quit talking and to listen.

Finding a quiet place to pray greatly helps us to become silent. One of the primary reasons that we find it difficult to hear the voice of the Holy Spirit is that there are so many other voices grabbing our attention. There are the voices of family and friends, the television and the telephone. There are the voices of the workplace, the neighborhood and even the church community. These aren't necessarily bad voices. But we must sometimes shut them out so we can be completely available to hear the voice of the Lord. We need to find a special place where there is uninterrupted exterior silence so we can hear God. (I have one friend who found a silent place only by going into her garage and locking herself in her car.)

But finding a silent place is only part of silence. Becoming silent within ourselves is the other part. The *voices* of our conscious concerns and even subconscious thoughts need to be calmed because they can *scream* so loudly that we will not hear the voice of the Holy Spirit.

We have some control over this by choosing where we focus our attention. We can begin prayer by repeating rote prayers such as the Our Father, or by looking at a crucifix or other symbol of God. We can gently repeat the name of Jesus, knowing it is He who calms our souls. We can read a psalm. Once we are calm, we can stop the verbal prayers and enter true silence of the soul.

Finally, we can call upon the Lord himself through his grace to help us move into a place of silence and calm. When we cannot bring ourselves to the needed interior silence, we can simply admit to God that we want to listen to him but cannot get beyond our own worries, fears and concerns. Doing so, we have opened the door for him to intervene on our behalf.

One of the obstacles to entering into both stillness and silence is the worldly fear that we might be wasting precious time. Especially when it sometimes seems as if nothing is happening in our prayr. I think at these moments it is helpful to imagine what God might be thinking. He is probably thinking how very wonderful it is that someone cares enough about him to just be in his presence. He is probably smiling.

SOLITUDE

Solitude means simply being alone, apart from other people. Solitude in prayer means simply being alone with oneself and with God.

Solitude is not the same as loneliness. Loneliness is a longing for the comforting presence of another. It can happen in a room filled with people. Take, for example a child flying alone to Grandma's for the first time on a crowded airplane. He is not alone but may be very lonely.

Solitude, on the other hand, implies being in a place without anyone else present where we may be perfectly at peace. You experience solitude without loneliness, for example, when you are in the shower!

Because we dread loneliness, it seems to me, we tend to avoid solitude. In doing so, however, we may miss the blessings of an intense personal encounter with our Lord. Moses received the Ten Commandments when he was alone on Mount Sinai. Jesus regularly went off into *lonely places* to pray, the Gospels tell us. Why not us ordinary Christians of the 21st century?

I suppose one reason we avoid solitude is that we doubt that there will be anything else to sustain us if we shut out our supporting network of people and daily activities. We doubt that our inner resources will be sufficient or that the presence of God can really be there. We wonder if anything spiritual can happen if there is not someone else there to help it happen. But often the Holy Spirit's voice within our soul becomes more recognizable when we are alone.

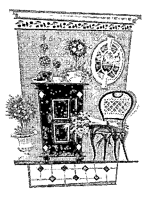

PRAYER EXERCISE TWO

(If you have never done this, it might be
the most important prayer exercise of all.)

Meditation:

When no one is at home, walk prayerfully through all the
rooms of your home. Consider which one might be a special
place for you to pray on a regular basis. Find a comfortable
chair or cushion. Place some religious symbols within sight of
your seat. Turn off the ringer if there is a phone in the room.
Close the blinds if people could look in at you. Close the door.
Pray!

*"But when you pray, go to your inner room, close the door
and pray to your Father in secret." (Matthew 6:5)*

Chapter Three

Awakening to His Voice

On rare occasions, God's voice is experienced audibly. In the Gospel, this happened dramatically at the baptism of Jesus in the Jordan River.

"After all the people had been baptized and Jesus also had been baptized and was praying, heaven was opened and the Holy Spirit descended upon him in bodily form like a dove. And a voice came from heaven, 'You are my beloved Son; with you I am well pleased.'" (Luke 3:21-22)

It happened again at the moment of Jesus' Transfiguration. Peter, James and John heard God's audible voice say, "This is my beloved Son. Listen to him." (Mark 9:7)

But it isn't just people in the Scriptures long ago who heard God's voice. People even now hear that voice. A woman I know recently told me that her family is financing the building of a Eucharistic Chapel for their local cathedral. She has had much of the responsibility for getting the project done and could not decide what would be the appropriate name for the chapel. She began seeking God in earnest prayer about the name. Before long she was awakened in the middle of the night with a loud voice that said, "Call it St. Michael." It was an audible voice, and she had no doubt who was talking!

Certainly God, who is all powerful, can use the extraordinary measure of a humanly audible voice to guide and direct us. Most often, however, He speaks through the voice of the Holy Spirit, who dwells within our souls. It is a quiet but powerful inner voice that is constantly knocking on the door of our hearts.

Many of us, unfortunately, have not understood how real and active is the help of the Holy Spirit in our personal lives, even though we are faithful church members. However, as we open our minds and hearts to this possibility, we can experience an *awakening* to the Holy Spirit's power. To explain what I mean by this, I am going to describe an awakening experience of mine which took place when I was a young adult and forever changed my life. Such experiences are personal and different for each of us, but I think that telling you mine will help to explain my point.

Until I was about 25, I did not believe that God had personally called me by name. Or, rather, I had not recognized his call even though I was a baptized Christian and a practicing Catholic convert. At the time I thought of God as the "big power out there somewhere." I did not think of him as close to me since I was just one of billions of human beings.

However, on one special occasion, I suddenly recognized God's closeness to me. It was a startling encounter. It happened while I was giving birth to one of our sons, right at the actual moment of his birth. At that beautiful moment when the doctor lifted my newborn son up for me to see, I saw something stunning.

Of course, I saw my son, perfectly formed and awesomely wonderful. But I saw something else with the eyes of my soul; I *saw* the presence of God. I saw the power of the Creator, bigger than the power of my husband and myself, through whom this child had been conceived and born. God had created a new human being with his own imprint, very personally and deliberately. And I felt the presence of God in the room at this moment of giving birth. It was a grace infused into my soul at an already dramatic moment in my life. Suddenly I recognized the God of the universe as someone who would personally speak to me and act in my own life.

Before this, I had regarded my relationship with God in somewhat the same way I understood my relationship with the president of the United States. He wasn't someone whom I could contact directly, nor would he know me as an individual.

Rather, he influenced my life because I was "one of the masses." His power to help was great, but not directed to me specifically.

Now, however, I was shocked to discover that somehow I could feel God's personal attention and blessing focused upon me. It really shook me up. In fact, as I returned to my hospital bed from the delivery room, I found myself on fire with an inner energy that I had never experienced. I lay in bed for hours unaffected by the sleeping medication the nurse had given me. I kept telling God "thank you" and "I love you," and then wondering to myself how all of a sudden I could be talking in such personal terms to God. I had never felt like this before. Suddenly I was aware of the presence of the Holy Spirit in my soul. And I could feel God communicating with me, not necessarily in human words, but with his loving presence.

Soon after my son was born, I went to meet with some people who told me they had received the Holy Spirit's gift of praying in tongues. I wanted to hear what that sounded like. At their meeting, as the group was laying hands on a woman who had asked to also receive the gift of tongues, one man present put his hand on my shoulder. Immediately, I again experienced being immersed in God's presence. I fell into a chair because I couldn't stand up in the power of this presence. I was conscious no longer of what was going on in the room but rather seemed to be what I can only describe as "out there somewhere in the presence of God." I returned home really wondering what was happening to me. First the experience with my son's birth, now this.

The next morning, after I fed my new baby son and while I was doing the breakfast dishes alone in the kitchen, I felt an overwhelming urge to give thanks to God for the good things He was doing for me. As I began to give thanks, strange words of praise in a language unfamiliar to me came forth from my mouth. I realized this was the gift of tongues. It had come to me even though I hadn't asked for it, from the Lord who was reaching out to me.

I went to the bookshelf in the family room and picked up a Bible, which I had received as a gift along with my diploma at my college graduation. I had not looked at it for the six years it had been in my possession. But at this moment, as I casually flipped it open to one of the Gospels, the words practically jumped off the page with life and meaning to me. Words that one day before would have seemed as dull to me as the classified ads in a newspaper all of a sudden made perfect sense and seemed to be speaking to me personally. The newly awakened Holy Spirit within my soul was connecting with the power of the Spirit in the words of Scripture. I felt immersed in the enveloping power of the Holy Spirit. It was like an electric charge. I knew at that point that God was somehow very near to me. And I began trying to listen to him speak because I realized that He was reaching out to me.

I talked to priests, to friends. I read any book I could find that talked about the spiritual life with the power of the Holy Spirit. I went to prayer groups and read the Bible, and began trying to listen to the Holy Spirit's inspiration. Since that time, He has been helping me and teaching me and even leading me to understand who He is.

If you are baptized, this same Holy Spirit lives within you. He is present and alive and wants to influence your life. If you listen for him, if you defer to his wisdom and make yourself open to his gifts, you will hear him.

I have mentioned my dog, Hannah. She is bright, affectionate and communicative. (She communicates by barking, nudging me, and by certain looks in her eyes.) In some ways she does what a human companion would do. But she is not human, that is to say, not a person. She is a dog.

Just as sheep can only be led by external guidance, the same is true for Hannah. I lead her by telling her things, by pushing or pulling her or inducing her to action with a treat. But Jesus, our Shepherd, can lead us from within our souls by the prompting of the Holy Spirit. Because we are persons, created in the image of God who is three persons! One of those three persons who is God — the Holy Spirit — lives in our souls and remains always present to our spirit.

This Holy Spirit quietly influences our thoughts and actions. Sometimes we do not even notice his prompting and influence so the Holy Spirit goes unrecognized even as He is helping us.

How many times have you looked back on some decision you've made and said, "Thank the Lord I made that choice. God must have been with me"? Or have you had the experience of sitting down with a friend who really needed someone to talk with and found just the right words coming from your heart to help that friend? And you wondered, "Where did those words come from?" Very likely it was the inspiration of the Holy Spirit.

He is given to us by God to communicate directly with us, to help and guide us. And this help is very great indeed. Even beyond silent prompting, He will, when He sees the need, speak with us, telling us the very things Jesus would want to tell us if He were visibly standing in our presence.

PRAYER EXERCISE THREE

Find a quiet place. Quiet your own spirit. Ask the Holy Spirit to help you now to put aside personal thoughts and concerns and to pray.

Meditation:

Picture yourself kneeling beside your bed. Imagine Jesus coming into your room and sitting on the edge of your bed. He invites you to sit beside him. "I want to talk to you about your life," He says. "We are in this together, you know. I am glad I found you in here on your knees asking for my help." Notice that Jesus begins to look right into your eyes. You sense that He has something important to say. He says, "Right now you see me with your eyes, but that will not always be so. Because of this, I am awakening within you my own divine Spirit. My Spirit will strengthen you on those days when you cannot see me sitting beside you as you do now. My Spirit will always help you just as I want to help you. He will tell you all that I want to tell you and He will inspire you and uplift you."

Jesus places his hand upon your heart and says, "Receive the graces of my Spirit within. Be blessed. You are a beloved child of my Father."

How do you respond?

> *"The Spirit remains with you and will be in you.*
> *I will not leave you orphans." (John 14:17-18)*

Chapter Four

Scripture Says We Can Hear God's Voice

In the Gospel, Jesus tells us we can hear his voice. He said, "My sheep hear my voice. I know them and they follow me. I give them eternal life, and they shall never perish." (John 10:27) But how do we hear his voice? Traditional Catholic Christianity has universally acknowledged that we can know his words by the words in Scripture and by the words of apostolic teaching. But what about hearing his voice directly? Why should we presume to believe that we can hear God speak personally to each one us?

Those who lived around Galilee 2,000 years ago heard the voice of God the Father speaking through Jesus the Son. They could hear his human voice. But to those of us who have lived after Jesus' ascension to heaven the power to hear the voice of God comes through the presence of the third part of the Trinity — the Holy Spirit. Jesus said, "The Advocate, the Holy Spirit that the Father will send in my name — He will teach you everything and remind you of all that I told you." (John 14:26)

The Bible itself records many instances of disciples hearing God's voice through the Holy Spirit. In the book of Acts we're told about Peter and Paul and other apostles hearing the voice of the Lord guiding them. In Acts, Chapter 8, for example, the story is told of Philip going to Ethiopia. On route, Philip passes an Ethiopian eunuch seated in his chariot reading from the book of Isaiah. Then, says the author of Acts, "The Spirit said to Philip, 'Go and join up with that chariot.'" (Acts 8:29) God was directing Philip directly through the voice of the Holy Spirit. Philip obeyed and the Ethiopian was evangelized and baptized.

Also in Acts the initial coming of the Holy Spirit into the hearts and minds of Jesus' disciples is vividly described. It happened following Jesus' ascension into heaven as the disciples gathered for prayer in Jerusalem in the same place where they had shared the Passover meal with Jesus before his crucifixion.

"When the day of Pentecost came, they were all together in one place. Suddenly a sound like the blowing of a violent wind came from heaven and filled the whole house where they were sitting. They saw what seemed to be tongues of fire that separated and came to rest on each of them. All of them were filled with the Holy Spirit and began to speak in other tongues as the Spirit enabled them." (Acts 2:1-4)

The skeptics watching this episode explained it away by saying that those touched by the Holy Spirit were just drunk. But Peter explained it using the words of the prophet Joel (who was speaking words he heard directly from God):

"It will come to pass in the last days," says God, "that I will pour out a portion of my spirit on all flesh. Your sons and your daughters shall prophesy, your young men shall see visions, your old men shall dream dreams. Indeed, upon my servants and my handmaids I will pour out a portion of my spirit in those days and they shall prophesy, and I will work wonders in the heavens above and signs on the earth below." (Acts 2:17-19)

What do people today need to hear God speak? The presence of the Holy Spirit. It is clear from examining the Scriptures that the power that enabled believers to hear God's voice 2,000 years ago was the Holy Spirit. It's the same for us today. The words of Peter to those gathered in Jerusalem at Pentecost apply to us now:

"Repent and be baptized, every one of you, in the name of Jesus Christ for the forgiveness of your sins; and you will receive the gift of the Holy Spirit. For the promise is made to you and to your children and to all those far off, whomever the Lord our God will call." (Acts 2:38-39)

PRAYER EXERCISE FOUR

Sit in a comfortable chair and rest peacefully in the knowledge of God's presence with you. As before, quiet yourself and ask the Holy Spirit to help you to pray.

Imagine Jesus entering the room. He sits in a chair near you and says, "I want you to think about those who have gone before you and are now with me in heaven. Think of Peter and Paul who lived around my time. Do you realize that they accomplished large tasks for the spread of the kingdom only because they were given my Holy Spirit? Are you aware that you too have received the same Holy Spirit that those early apostles received? Just as I gave them power, strength, and wisdom for their tasks, I give help to you for your tasks.

"Will you accept the help the Holy Spirit offers to you to do our Father's will? Will you yield to his promptings?"

What is your response?

"He saved us through the bath of rebirth and renewal by the Holy Spirit, whom He richly poured out on us through Jesus Christ our Savior." (2 Timothy 3:5-6)

Chapter Five

The Holy Spirit's Supernatural Power

I f we open our hearts to the presence of God and the power of the Holy Spirit, the Spirit can intervene in our lives in many extraordinary ways. Even in little ways just known to us alone. Let me give you a few examples from my own life:

Several years ago I was praying early in the morning. As I passed by my front door and looked out the window, I saw a fallen palm branch on my front porch. The thought crossed my mind that the branch looked a lot like a snake, even though I knew it was only a branch. But the snake impression was so strong (I fear snakes) that I opened my front door and removed the dead palm branch. About two hours later, as I opened my front door to go out to my car, I found, sitting in the exact same spot on my front porch, a real living snake the same color as the palm branch! I have never, in the twenty years I have lived in our home, seen a snake on the front porch or even in the grass. This was no coincidence. I believe the Holy Spirit alerted me that a snake was going to be on my porch by planting the idea in my mind that the branch was a snake. He was protecting me in a simple, small way by forewarning me. It really helped. When I saw the actual snake, I did not panic although I was surprised by the sequence of events.

Here's another example. One night I dreamed that my two cocker spaniel dogs were driving my car. The next day, forgetting my dream, I drove over to drop a book at a friend's house and brought the dogs along. I spent a few minutes talking with my friend, leaving the dogs in the car. Suddenly, my friend's teenage son burst in the front door and cried out, "Mrs. Marquardt, come look at your dogs. They're both at the steering wheel of your car and it looks like they're trying to drive!" We even quickly took a photo, which I still have. There is no natural explanation that I am aware of for this strange intermingling of reality and my dream. I believe the Holy Spirit was speaking symbolically to me through this experience, reinforcing the message of the dream by a real life experience. The message was: Your emotions (symbolized by the dogs) are steering your life (symbolized by driving the car) right now. It was again a simple prompting, this time alerting me to what was going on inside myself.

Sometimes in prayer when I am just *listening* and being with the Lord, the Holy Spirit shows me, in my imagination, the faces of people I know. I always assume that I am being shown that person's face because he or she needs special prayer. On one such occasion, I saw the face of a young man who was a college classmate of my son. I began praying for this young man and continued for several days. Then one evening my son called from college just to see how we were doing. I asked him in the course of the conversation whether anything was wrong with the young man for whom I'd been praying. I told him I had seen the friend's face in prayer. My son laughed and told me I was only imagining this. The friend was fine.

The next night my son called back to tell me that, after hanging up the phone the previous evening, his friend had come knocking on his dormitory door and asked him to go out for a snack. The two went and the friend began to pour out his heart to my son, describing a problem that had him tied up in knots. To this day I do not know what the problem was, but I do know that when my son told the friend about his phone conversation with me, it did wonders to encourage the young man. He figured that if God had shown his face in prayer to a lady many miles away in Florida, then God was aware and concerned about his problem. He could have faith that there would be a solution. And I was so glad that I had listened! It taught me that if I'm listening, God can use me in ways I don't even ask to be used. And He intervenes to show us the things He wants us to do.

These examples confirm to me that the power of the Holy Spirit is dynamic and what I would call *supernatural*. When we think of the spirit within us, we first think of our own human spirit, which is created in the image and likeness of God. It is a natural, not supernatural, spirit. This created spirit of ours is where our instincts and drives and emotions originate. These have power to motivate and direct our lives. But the Holy Spirit is not us. He is a personal power living in us that is not our own. He is God dwelling within us, apart and different from our natural human spirit. The Holy Spirit provides God's wisdom and love.

It is important to recognize that the spirits of two autonomous beings live within the soul of us baptized Christians: our own natural human spirit and God's supernatural Holy Spirit. Once we decide to surrender to the authority of God in this life, He intervenes in supernatural ways to help us. For some reason we think this odd or unlikely. But remember that God in heaven is spirit and beyond the natural as we know it. So his help can have supernatural origins and sometimes supernatural manifestations.

PRAYER EXERCISE FIVE

Begin as in previous exercises by finding a quiet place and a quiet time. Ask the Holy Spirit to bring to your mind times when He has helped you.

Meditation:

Make a list of two or three times when something has happened in your life that really helped you but that you yourself did not make happen.

1. _____

2. _____

3. _____

Close your eyes and imagine each of these events, one at a time. Ask Jesus to show you whether it was the Holy Spirit helping. Wait for a sense about whether the answer is *yes* or *no*. You may be able to tell because a deeper insight into the meaning of that event will come into your mind. Or you may just get a *knowing sense* of a *yes* or a *no*.

Tell the Lord your own feelings regarding these events.

"For everyone who asks, receives." (Luke 11:10)

Chapter Six

God's Personal Invitation
to Relationship

Several years ago I was in prayer one morning when it dawned on me that Father's Day was just two days away. I had forgotten about it and had no gift for my husband, Mark. I got an idea at that very moment: a rocking chair for our porch. Mark had been wanting one.

I prayed, "Lord, you know how little time I have for shopping in the next few days. Could you please help me?" It was a little thing to ask of God. Little, first, in the sense that it might seem like a trivial thing to ask of God, who has the big problems of the universe. Little, second, in that it was a relatively small personal thing for me to ask him as compared, for instance, with solving a major family problem.

Anyway I said those words in prayer probably as much out of anxiety about how I was going to solve the problem as in expectation of an answer. But within an instant there flashed into my mind the picture of a furniture store that was near my neighborhood but not a place where I had ever shopped or would have thought to go. It struck me that this might actually be the Lord answering my prayer with some guidance because I knew I would never have thought of this particular store. So later in the day, when I was near the store anyway, I stopped in.

To my surprise, there was a sign on the store window saying, "Going out of business sale." I went in and started browsing, not seeing any rockers. Just to be sure, I asked a salesclerk if there were any rocking chairs for sale. She said, "Yes, there is one in the back room of the store." She brought it out to show me. It was exactly what I was looking for, and it was on sale at 40 percent off!

I knew then for sure that the Holy Spirit had helped me. It wasn't important in the big scheme of things for God, but He wanted to help me out when I asked. After all, you or I would do the same for a friend if we had the answer. That day God treated me like a friend. I was reminded that God will *bother* with the little things because he's our friend. There is enough love and power in him to answer small as well as large problems.

Is it a little delusional to believe that God would want to talk with me when I'm just one small human being in a vast universe? Not at all. When He speaks to us, the most important thing He says is that He wants a living relationship with us. Because God is spirit, He can be present to each of us no matter where we are.

When the disciples asked Jesus how to pray to God, He told them to address God as one would affectionately address his or her earthly father. (Luke, Chapter 11) The author of the New Testament letters of John reaffirms that understanding. He tells us, "See what love the Father has bestowed on us that we may be called the children of God. Yet so we are." (1 John 3:1)

Jesus told his followers to think of him as a friend. "You are my friends if you do what I command you," Jesus said, "I no longer call you slaves, because a slave does not know what his master is doing. I have called you friends because I have told you everything I have heard from my Father." (John 15:14-15)

We have been given an invitation to a loving and intimate relationship with God the Father and Jesus! Think about this in human terms. In a friendship we expect the other person to provide some sort of companionship, support and help. And we do the same in return. Although we may never verbalize these expectations and the intention to meet them for one another, they still form the basis for trust, which makes the interaction between us a *friendship*. We are present to each other and come to know one another more deeply.

By contrast, when we are in trouble, we may be helped out

or supported by someone who is a kind stranger. An example might be a passerby who stops to change a flat tire. We interact with that person in a meaningful way at a particular moment, yet there is no real relationship between us, no friendship. The other person has helped us, but between us there is nothing ongoing, no expectations or trust. I recall one kind couple who invited me into their home once to call for help when I had a flat tire while on a vacation. I still recall and appreciate their kindness but I don't even know their names. I could not call them my friends.

Sometimes I wonder if we aren't tempted to treat Jesus, our saving Lord, as a helper who is a passerby rather than a friend. We are content to let him help us in a bind, and certainly want him to appear to forgive us and get us into heaven at the hour of death — much like a person stopping to help us change a flat tire. There's no lasting commitment.

Jesus, however, has a much different plan in mind. He intends to be with us always, as He promised in the Gospels. He promises to forgive us constantly whenever we ask. He invites us to a personal friendship with him. In responding to his invitation to personal relationship, we talk to him. But He gave us the Holy Spirit so we can also listen to him!

PRAYER EXERCISE SIX

After finding a quiet time and spot, think back to when you were a child. Try to recall the name of a favorite childhood friend. Think of events or activities that made your friendship important.

Then, recall your teenage years. Think of someone who was a real friend to you in those years. Recall the strength and encouragement your friend brought to you.

Name of a childhood friend: _____

Name of a teenage friend: _____

Meditation:

Talk with Jesus in your mind, asking him how his friendship with you is like your childhood friendship and your teenage friendship. Also, ask how his friendship might be different.

"I have called you friends because I have told you everything I have heard from my Father." (John 15:15)

Chapter Seven

Prayer Builds Relationship

The first time I remember being asked on a "date," I was with my family at the beach for a holiday weekend. I was 11 years old and the son of my parents' friends, who was 13, asked me to go for a walk on the boardwalk. I can still remember the thrill and excitement I felt that he invited me to go with him, that he liked me enough to ask me. The spirit of romance lifted me and brought me great excitement.

My date was a simple thing. We walked along the boardwalk and then stopped in a little soda shop. We ordered one chocolate soda with two straws, and we sipped that soda together and then returned home.

The joy and good feelings of that simple experience stayed with me for a long time, and I can still recall it now, more than 40 years later. I can't remember a bit of the conversation we had, just the thrill of the experience of being on a romantic date.

This is somewhat the way I felt when Jesus' presence came into my life experientially. I knew then that He had singled me out and invited me to go with him on a long walk through this life. The joy of his presence was thrilling and sufficient in itself at the time — the simple joy of being with Jesus lifted me.

But that was only the beginning of my relationship with Jesus. If that had been the whole substance, it would have had little more effect upon my present life than that childhood date.

The better analogy for my full relationship with the Lord is probably my relationship with my husband. Mark has truly mirrored Jesus' love for me in a profound and lasting way. Mark came into my life through a blind date at college ten years after my "boardwalk date." He had a beautiful sparkle in his eyes and a strong, gentle presence. For me, it was love at first sight. Today he still has the sparkle and gentle presence, but our relationship is very different.

The excitement of the beginning has long gone, although I can remember it. Instead, *just being together* has become a deep and important part of our relationship. I draw a sustaining strength and peace from it. There are many times when we sit in the same room and read or work on our individual projects. Or go for a walk silently together. Or eat a meal with only a few words. (But believe me, in order to reach this stage of being together we have had plenty of words and conversations during the 34 years we have been married!)

My prayer relationship with Jesus seems to me a lot like my relationship with Mark, even though my initial experience with him was sort of like a boardwalk date sipping a soda with two straws. Since that powerful experience of God more than 25 years ago at the birth of my son, the thirst for knowing God more fully has not left me. And as I have sought him, I have learned to listen and to pray. He and I have done a lot of talking.

After my initial experiences of becoming aware of the Holy Spirit's presence I began to take time for quiet prayer. I reached out to God who had really reached out to me. After my initial experiences with the Holy Spirit, I knew I had to keep going with God.

At first, I read a lot of books and listened to many teachers and friends. But looking back, I think I mostly learned to interact with the Holy Spirit by practice, which means by prayer.

I don't mean rote prayers we may have learned as children, but a continual two-way conversation between me and God. After all, He created me with a specific purpose in mind. So when I realized how close He really was, how accessible, I started talking and listening. I gave up other things that might have occupied this time period every day just to focus on the Lord. Prayer became something altogether different than I had ever known or expected. It was something life-giving, consoling and exciting!

Earlier in my life, I had thought of personal prayer as only a wishful hoping out loud with the possibility that a higher being might exist and help. I didn't do it much unless I was feeling desperate. After all, what value did wishing have other than revealing to me what I lacked and creating feelings of inadequacy and frustration? However, when I realized that prayer is not wishing but authentic seeking and communicating, things really changed for me.

I found that living in the presence of the Lord required intimate dialogue with him. I talked. God listened. God talked. I listened. Trying this, on occasion, I got downright obnoxious in my requests, but shockingly, sometimes the Lord answered anyway. I remember one time when my older son was running a high fever. I was scared. I said out loud to the Lord, "Jesus, why don't you do something about this?" To my amazement, when I went back into my son's room, his fever had broken — not to return. This experience helped to teach me not to hesitate to bring whatever is in my heart before the Lord. Let him respond according to his wisdom. (After all, He knows everything in our hearts anyway.)

Jesus, himself, is the perfect model for intimate personal prayer. The Gospels tell of Jesus often going away to a lonely place to pray to his Father. Undoubtedly, Jesus poured out his heart to his Father. He must have listened carefully because each time He rejoined the disciples, He seemed to know what his Father wanted him to do and say. And He seemed to know with certainty what his Father was like.

Once a few years ago, Mark and I were spending a quiet weekend at a remote cabin on the Withlacoochee River in central Florida. Father Justin, a priest friend of ours, came by to visit and offered to celebrate Mass with us. Before long, there came a knock on our door. I opened it to a young woman accompanied by a younger man and a boy, all rather shy looking. The woman began to tell me about God Jehovah and offered me a magazine. I said that I was a Catholic and, in fact, was in the midst of celebrating Eucharist with my husband and a priest friend. I invited her to come in for prayer, but she got a frightened look on her face, stuck the magazine hastily inside her bag, urged her two friends back to their car and said, "Thanks. Why don't you just pray for us?"

I imagine it likely that a culturally imposed fear of Catholicism sent this young woman scurrying away. But the reality was that she came to my door to talk about God and left in a hurry when I suggested she actually sit down at the table with him in a Eucharistic celebration.

To me, prayer is not unlike answering an invitation to an intimate meal with the Lord. It is a leisurely repast with time to savor the food as well as the company, and to relax together afterward.

In the Gospels, Jesus called Zacchaeus the tax collector down out of a sycamore tree and went to his home to share his dinner. We can only imagine what tender and healing expressions of friendship between the two went on at this meal. This story is a good model of what goes on between us and the Lord when we respond to his call to personal relationship — the intimacy with him, the unexpected surprises, the dawning light of his truth in our hearts.

Over the years, I have spent much time in prayer dialogue with the Lord. The Holy Spirit has taught me a lot about what God is like and what He wants from me. He has also taught me a lot about myself. His quiet and gentle words of love and forgiveness, his persistent prodding and prompting, his consolation in difficult times and his wisdom in confusing times have changed my life and my heart. He has given me wonderful sustenance and peace.

PRAYER EXERCISE SEVEN

Find a quiet place to sit in silence. Ask the Holy Spirit to guide you in this time of prayer.

Meditation:

Imagine this scene: You are sitting in a pew at church. Jesus himself walks down from the front of the church to your pew and looks just at you. He says, "Today I would really like to visit your home. Could I join you for lunch?"

You respond...

If you said yes, imagine Jesus going home with you. Where would you invite him to sit? What would you serve him for lunch?

Imagine sitting down after lunch is on the table and having a conversation. This is your chance to say the things you really want to tell him and ask the things you really want to ask him.

How does your conversation go?

"Jesus looked up quickly and said, 'Zacchaeus, come down, for today I must stay at your house.'" (Luke 19:5)

Chapter Eight

The Holy Spirit Brings
Personal Revelation

I use the term *personal revelation* to describe the insights and awareness that the Holy Spirit gives to me. I mean by this that God is revealing personally to me the things I need to know and understand from the gospel message and from present life circumstances in order to live a life consistent with his plan. He is giving me personal insights from his point of view. It is *revelation* because the Holy Spirit is showing me something I could not see on my own.

Do you ever have the experience of hearing a gospel teaching and not understanding what it means? No wonder, because the spiritual truths revealed by Jesus cannot be fully grasped by the human mind alone. The most learned of us cannot grasp what Jesus came to teach without the help of the Holy Spirit because his message includes divine revelation, that is, teaching from beyond human experience. His teaching embraces an eternal vision that surpasses the grasp of the human mind.

Look at what Jesus himself said about understanding the things of God:

"I give you praise Father, Lord of heaven and earth, for although you have hidden these things from the wise and the learned, you have revealed them to the childlike. Yes, Father, such has been your gracious will. All things have been handed over to me by my Father. No one knows who the Son is except the Father, and who the Father is except the Son and anyone to whom the Son wishes to reveal him." (Luke 10:21-22)

Right before telling the reader this, Luke tells us that Jesus, "rejoiced in the Holy Spirit." He knew that it was the Holy Spirit from the Father that actually revealed these truths to people who were childlike, who were trusting and receptive.

Today, also, God in the person of the Holy Spirit will reveal to each of us personally the meaning of the gospel words we read and the gospel truths we are taught if we listen attentively to him. He will teach us what our human minds cannot grasp.

There is another reason why listening to the Holy Spirit is important in reading Scripture. The Gospels must be understood by our entire being, not only our mind. Without such a grasp, our mind can misinterpret what has been taught. Only when gospel teaching sinks into our inner being (which Scripture refers to as our *heart*) does it have the power to move us and change us in attitudes and vision. Only when it sinks into our *heart* can we begin to really understand the love that God has for us and offers us daily.

A prayer experience recently told me by a friend illustrates this principle that the Holy Spirit is the great teacher of our heart.

My friend was reading Scriptures during her quiet prayer time. She was meditating upon the passage about Jesus praying in the Garden of Gethsemane just prior to his betrayal by Judas and his arrest. She said she was deeply struck by the words, "Father, if it be possible, let this cup pass me by, but not my will but yours be done." (Luke 22:42) She stopped reading and pondered these words. Suddenly she was unexpectedly overcome with sorrow and love for Jesus. She began to sob uncontrollably.

At first, she did not know what had come over her for she had read this passage many times before without such a reaction. But reflecting for a while after her emotions calmed down, she realized that at that particular time she had heard with her *heart* that Jesus was truly human. She realized how He had suffered as we suffer, only worse, for love of us. She understood in a new, different way how Jesus was really like us in his capacity to feel and to be hurt and how much He really cared for us. This profound understanding moved her to tears.

Something new and deep and beautiful had been personally revealed to her as she read Scripture prayerfully. She was already well aware of the teachings that Jesus was truly human and that He loved us dearly. However, at a particular graced moment, the Holy Spirit brought the deep experience of this truth to her *heart*. She says she will henceforth relate to Jesus in an entirely new way, even though she has been a believer since childhood.

There is a Scripture passage that always stirs my soul no matter how often I read it, and I relate to it this idea of personal revelation. It is commonly referred to as the Canticle of Zechariah and is found in the first chapter of the Gospel of Luke.

It is the proclamation of joy spoken by Zechariah when he witnesses the circumcision of his newborn son, John the Baptist, eight days after his birth. I'm sure Zechariah was overjoyed at the birth of his one and only son because he had waited a very long time. Luke tells us that he was an old man and that his wife, Elizabeth, was also advanced in age and barren.

The part of Zechariah's proclamation that always stirs my heart says, "In the tender mercy of our God, the dawn from on high will break upon us to shine on those who dwell in darkness and the shadow of death and guide our feet into the way of peace." (Luke 1:78-79)

When I read these words of Zechariah's now, they remind me that Jesus' coming means we all need not live in the darkness of ignorance about God and despair about death. Rather the bright light and hope of Jesus has broken into our lives. His light through the Holy Spirit dawns within our souls bringing us awareness of his love and knowledge of his intended destiny for us. This is glorious and it is life-giving for us.

I recognize these words of Zechariah as a foreshadowing not only of the coming of Jesus in the flesh, but of the coming of the power of the Holy Spirit to us, Jesus' followers. It is the dawning of the heavenly life upon our earthly hearts.

It is the Holy Spirit who inspired the Scripture writers with the biblical truths. It is the Holy Spirit who inspires our religious leaders to continue to lead us to the truths of the Gospel. These are truly the 'dawn from on high' breaking into our minds. However, it is prayer, dialogue with the Lord in the power of the

Holy Spirit, that brings these same truths to our *hearts.*

We need authoritative teaching to bring truth to our minds and prayer to bring truth to our hearts. Truth in our hearts has the power to overcome the temptations of our human nature to rebel against the truths in our minds.

The book of Hebrews describes this reality:

"The Holy Spirit also testifies to us: 'This is the covenant I will establish with them after those days, says the Lord: I will put my laws in their hearts, and I will write them upon their minds.'" (Hebrews 10:15-16)

When we hear the voice of God in personal prayer, we will not be told something different than that which has already been publicly revealed in Christianity. The Holy Spirit will not reveal a new gospel or any sort of change from the full revelation given in Jesus 2,000 years ago. What we'll hear is the deeper meaning of the Gospel and its personal relevance to our own situations in life.

Each of us can hear the Shepherd's voice through Scripture, through Church teaching, through our pastoral leaders. But we also hear his voice most lovingly and personally in the depths of our own being wherein dwells the Holy Spirit.

PRAYER EXERCISE EIGHT

Go to a quiet spot as usual. Spend a few minutes telling the Lord of your love for him and whatever feelings are in your heart.

Meditation:

Then, think of a familiar gospel story, one you can go over in your mind without reading it in the Bible. Possibly choose the Christmas story or a parable such as the shepherd searching for a lost sheep. Go over the story in your mind. Try to picture it unfolding in your imagination.

Sit quietly a few minutes, then think over the story again, asking the Holy Spirit to give you deeper personal understanding of its meaning.

"But blessed are your eyes because they see and your ears because they hear." (Matthew 13:16)

Chapter Nine

The Guiding Voice of the Holy Spirit

Those of us following Jesus probably have this in common: we want to live a life of goodness, filled with meaning, that brings blessings to others as well as ourselves. We have recognized that the gospel offers us the guide map for such a life. And the Holy Spirit's guiding voice is such a wonderful gift in following the map.

Should I take this job or that? Should I be a stay at home mom or help earn some money for education expenses? What could I best do to help my friend in need? For all such questions the Lord leaves the decision to us. But sometimes his wisdom is a tremendous help. Just as a shepherd wisely steers his sheep toward pastures with green grass, the Holy Spirit guides us toward the most fruitful choices.

A few months after my initial awakening to the power and help of the Holy Spirit, I began to realize that God was providing this help so I would follow his guidance. He had some better plans for me than I had for myself! He, in fact, meant to determine the course of my life according to a higher wisdom than mine, if I was willing to cooperate. But He was asking for a certain surrender on my part. I would say simply that I became aware deep within myself that this surrender was necessary to live out my calling as a follower of Jesus. In this case, I did not hear specific words; I just developed a deep intuitive sense of what the Holy Spirit was asking.

I was going to have to choose many times to walk on God's

path for my life and allow the Holy Spirit to mold my thoughts and emotions in a new way, sometimes without understanding why. It was a little scary. But I knew what Jesus had taught, "Whoever does not take up his cross and follow after me is not worthy of me. Whoever finds his life will lose it and whoever loses his life for my sake will find it." (Matthew 10:38-39)

So one day I decided to willingly consecrate my life to Jesus, as I had been consecrated to him by my parents at my baptism. While my baby son and my toddler son were both napping, and I also was lying down to rest, I went to prayer. I summoned forth all my courage and said, "Okay, Jesus, I give my life to you." I really meant it, although I was a little apprehensive about what my promise might entail.

Immediately after saying this prayer, I experienced a distinct physical sensation of becoming a heavy, dead weight. My body felt as if it could not have been lifted off the bed where I rested if ten strong men had tried. That sensation lasted a few minutes and then passed. But it left me really mystified, and a little frightened. It was a long time before I ever told anyone about it because I feared they might think I was losing my mind. Eventually, I came to understand that this sensation was given to me by the Holy Spirit to emphasize that I was, in a sense, *dead* to my own plans for my life and *alive* to the Lord's plans. I was still a woman, a wife and a mother, but in numerous ways my life was changing direction. And I had now given God permission to rule my destiny! That was almost thirty years ago and I am not at all sorry I did this. Among other reasons, I believe it was the key to receiving the many graces the Lord has given me since.

Recently I took a walk on the beach to watch the sunset. The sky became scarlet and magenta as the sun slipped below the horizon of the Gulf of Mexico. Little children were playing in the sand as their parents absorbed the beauty in the sky... What has humanity ever created to match sunsets and babies? Why do we think we can make plans and projects that are better than God's? Or improve on God's intentions for our lives? It was truly a gift of the Holy Spirit those many years ago that moved my heart to surrender to the Lord. A far greater gift than I could imagine at the time.

PRAYER EXERCISE NINE

After getting into a quiet, prayerful place, consider whether you have actually committed your life to the plan of God for you. If you are not sure, ask the Holy Spirit to help you see.

Meditation:

If you so choose, pray the following prayer or something similar in your own words:

My Lord Jesus, I know that you have come to earth, died, and risen again to save me from eternal destruction and bring me into the loving hands of God. I thank you so very much.

I truly want to respond to this supreme love from you by giving my will and my life to the Father's plan and desires for me. I surrender all into your hands, Dear Lord, trusting in your love, mercy and eternal wisdom.

For now and forever I belong to you, the Father, and the Holy Spirit. Amen.

"The Father and I are one." (John 10:30)

PART TWO:
Hearing His Voice

Chapter Ten

How We Hear Him

During the last decades of the 20th century, there were many people all over the world claiming to receive messages from God for humanity. Many have been warning about forthcoming world events and disasters, which are a consequence of ignoring God's voice. All the messages contain an urgent plea to turn back to God. Only time and events will prove the authenticity of these various messages. But one thing we can believe for sure is that God wants us to turn to him and listen to him. He has given us the Holy Spirit to help us.

Since technological developments in communication have made it possible for people at opposite ends of the earth to communicate with each other, we should certainly not find it too hard to believe that the all-powerful God in heaven can communicate in the present moment with us. If He so chooses, He can send visible and audible messages. He made sight. He made sound. Just as He inspired the Bible and raised up the Church, He can communicate with each of us. What we need is faith and a heart ready to listen and to recognize and do God's will.

My husband and I go to our cabin in the woods about once a month to get away from our routine and relax, reflect and pray. It is often during these quiet, relaxing times that I most clearly recognize what the voice of the Shepherd is saying to me.

Sometimes we leave home at different times or from different places and so we drive in separate cars. One weekend some years ago, when we had two cars with us, we decided to stop for dinner on the drive home. But we didn't decide where we would stop before we left our cabin. As we were driving along the interstate, I saw a place where I wanted to stop. I tooted the horn, but Mark was listening to the radio and didn't hear me. I couldn't get his attention.

Suddenly I remembered that I had my new cell phone in the car. It was my first such phone and I was just getting accustomed to using it. Mark had a phone in his car because of work. I realized that I could call him on the telephone in the car! This was really a revolutionary idea to me at the time.

But there was a problem — I didn't know Mark's phone number. It was so frustrating. We ended up driving all the way home and eating scrambled eggs for dinner.

Mark and I had tools in our cars so that we could communicate with each other. But we lacked the necessary knowledge to use them. This is sometimes how it is with us and God. Awareness of how to communicate, especially how to hear him, is missing from our life of faith.

I am going to suggest to you some ways the Holy Spirit may communicate with you. I encourage you to test them for yourself.

PRAYER EXERCISE TEN

Imagine yourself taking a walk along a quiet, tree-lined road. You realize that Jesus is walking beside you. He tells you, "Please believe that it has never been my Father's intention to leave you in life alone and without our help. That is truly why the gift of prayer is such a great gift for us and for you. That is why the Holy Spirit given you is such a priceless treasure. You are never really alone. My Spirit is with you. Pray and become more aware of this presence."

Meditation:

In your imagination in prayer, reach out your hand to Jesus. Touch his hand. Ask him how you can become more receptive to the Holy Spirit.

In your heart, try to understand his response to your words.

"I will not leave you orphans. I will come to you." John 14:18)

Chapter Eleven

Listening in Scripture

One of the more obvious places to go to hear God's voice is the Bible. Christians believe that God has spoken definitively there and that the messages and stories in the Bible are the resounding voice of God. We regard the recorded words of Jesus in the Bible as God the Father's very words, because Jesus said He came only to reveal what the Father told him. He said, "I do nothing on my own, but I only say what the Father taught me." (John 8:28)

Similarly, along with Jews, we believe that the laws we call the Ten Commandments, which were given to Moses on Mount Sinai and recorded in the Old Testament, came from God directly.

These teachings from Scripture apply to all of us and therefore to each one of us personally. We can call them God's *word universal*, to all people of all time. This means these teachings apply directly and personally to each and every person. For example, Jesus said, "Blessed are the merciful for they will be shown mercy." This teaching from his Sermon on the Mount applies to you and to me, as well as to the crowd in Galilee to whom He said this directly two thousand years ago. It even applies to the people who are not yet born but will come after us. It is God's universal word through Jesus for all time.

But besides listening to God's universal message in the Bible, there is another way of experiencing Scripture — as the instrument of God's individual word to you *personally*. The Holy

Spirit will emphasize to you a particular line or passage that has a direct relevance to you at a given moment in your life. Then you know that a Scripture verse or passage is being used by the Lord to address you individually for your need or benefit. In a sense, you are hearing a particular word from Jesus.

Here is an example of what I mean. After my discovery of a personal relationship with Jesus and beginning a prayer life, I found myself getting panicky about what others might think of me now that I was becoming *religious*. It betrayed the code of my secular humanist friends. I was very worried that I would lose all my friends and be branded a religious fanatic.

At that particular time, it happened that practically every time I just randomly opened the New Testament, I would find myself on the same page, at the story of the raising of Jairus' daughter from the dead. And one line in particular would stand out to me as if it were underlined. "Fear is useless, what is needed is trust." (Luke 8:50)

After I randomly opened the Bible and it opened to this same passage several times, I realized that the Lord was speaking just those words to me personally. The passage had no meaning for me at that moment about a daughter dying. (I don't even have a daughter and I didn't know anyone whose daughter was dying.) Rather, it was the Holy Spirit's way of telling me how to approach my concern about rejection by friends. The way was to trust God and not to allow anxiety into my heart. God would provide for me. And, of course, He did. The subtle insults and innuendoes I did experience only strengthened me and drew me closer to the Lord. And the few friends who did abandon me were not friends I needed anyway!

But the point is, the Holy Spirit consoled and guided me by somehow bringing that passage to my attention over and over again: "Fear is useless, what is needed is trust." At that time, the Scripture was bringing me God's *word personal* rather than his *word universal*.

When we study the Bible, we are trying to understand the meaning of the teachings and their relevance to our personal lives. We are absorbing God's word universal as a help for our own spiritual journey in this life. But we can also prayerfully read a Scripture passage with openness to God's word personal, that is, his particular message to me at that moment in time communicated through the words of the Scriptures.

In this approach to hearing God's word, you choose or allow someone else to recommend a particular Scripture passage. But when you read it, you read it with the ears of your heart listening for a personal meaning as well as your mind thinking about what the passage says.

Sometimes, when doing this, a particular line in a Scripture passage will capture your attention. It may seem to have more emphasis for you than the rest of the passage. Or it may seem to your heart as if that line is in bold print. It just seems to stand out. If that happens, then ask the Holy Spirit in your heart to bring understanding to your mind about what the Lord wants you to see or understand through that particular line.

Once I was directing a middle-aged woman on a silent retreat. After asking the Holy Spirit for guidance, I suggested for her next meditation the story about Susanna at the end of the book of Daniel. This long passage tells the story of a young woman who was accosted in the garden of her home by two elderly men looking for sexual favors. She screamed for help. When help arrived, however, the two men accused her of trying to seduce them. The story continues as Daniel arrives on the scene and by his wit and wisdom tricks the men in their testimony so that the truth comes out. Susanna is exonerated and the two men are put to death for perjury.

When the woman on retreat read through this passage, she stopped suddenly when she reached the line, "Oh Lord, you know what is hidden and are aware of all things before they come to be: you know that they have testified falsely against me." (Daniel 13:42) Suddenly back into her conscious mind came a childhood memory, long ago repressed, of being falsely accused of stealing something.

She couldn't bring herself to meditate further on the plight of Susanna because she was overwhelmed with a flood of emotions regarding her own childhood experience. Reflecting back prayerfully on that experience during her retreat as an adult, talking it over with me, her retreat director, and prayerfully surrendering that still painful memory to Jesus, this woman experienced an extraordinary healing which left her much less fearful of being misjudged by others. Her life since has reflected a new interior peace.

On a retreat, when she was not expecting it, the Holy Spirit had spoken to her through a sentence from Scripture to bring forth for healing a painful, repressed memory. And she was truly given a gift of peace. She had experienced in a very meaningful way the *word personal.*

PRAYER EXERCISE ELEVEN

Read slowly through the following lines from the Old Testament book of Isaiah:

> But now, thus says the Lord,
> who created you, O Jacob, and formed you, O Israel:
> Fear not, for I have redeemed you;
> I have called you by name: you are mine.
> When you pass through the water, I will be with you;
> in the rivers you shall not drown.
> When you walk through fire, you shall not be burned;
> the flames shall not consume you.
> For I am the Lord your God,
> the Holy One of Israel, your Savior.
>
> (Isaiah 43:1-3)

Notice which line seems to be *speaking* to you, that is, which seems to stand out from the others when you read the passage.

Reflect prayerfully about why this line may have a personal meaning for you at this time.

Speak to Jesus in your mind about this line.

"For I have redeemed you." (Isaiah 43:1)

Chapter Twelve

Listening Through Your Imagination

When I was a young child, I had an imaginary friend named "Bodren." I only remember this vaguely but my parents have told me that I spent many happy hours playing alone with "Bodren." One of our sons had three imaginary playmates called "Gicki," "Picky" and "Jennifer." Mark and I would watch with amusement as our son interacted with these playmates, real enough at the time to him. Once when we were visiting with my parents in their condo, he "locked 'Gicki' in jail." This meant he locked the bedroom door from the inside, came out and closed the door. We were all locked out of that room, and we had to call a security guard to get the door unlocked. It was the closest to reality that his imaginary friend ever came!

"Bodren" existed only in my imagination as a child. "Gicki", "Picky" and "Jennifer" lived only in my son's imagination. They had no real existence apart from this. They were created in our minds at a specific time for specific emotional needs and then dissipated. They were in no sense real persons. Most of the time, when we speak of using imagination, it is in this sense of interiorly envisioning otherwise nonexistent things.

But imagination can be used as a tool to envision experiences and places that are real. For example, my husband and I recently have been planning a trip to France. Our imaginations have helped us plan our itinerary. By imagining what it would be like in different places in France, we have been able to choose the places we want to visit.

And our imaginations are helping us enjoy the trip before we actually go. We can picture ourselves driving into small villages and poking around. We can almost taste the French wine. We can think of ourselves in prayer in the grotto at Lourdes and draw joy from it. These experiences aren't real yet — but they will be before long. These images are extending the enjoyment of the trip.

Another way we use our imagination in connection with reality is to grasp the meaning of things that are really present but not visible. We speak of germs and imagine a germ in our mind, although we don't know what a germ actually looks like because it is too small to see. Similarly, we talk of atoms and galaxies. These we visualize for the sake of relating to them even though we can't physically capture their appearance.

If we can imagine what such real things as germs and galaxies look like, why not imagine what God looks like. God is very real. We just don't see his visible being with our physical eyes. So while our image in our mind certainly is not exactly what God looks like, it serves as a means of relating to him as a person.

The relevance of this to listening prayer is that we can allow the Holy Spirit to speak to us through the faculty of our imagination. Since He does not have a human physical or verbal presence, only a spiritual one, we give him our imagination as a tool for telling us what He wants us to hear and showing us what He wants us to see. The Holy Spirit can send us real messages through our imagination — in the form of words we hear or pictures we see in our minds. And the message the Holy Spirit sends is real, not imaginary.

Once in prayer I saw the face of a young man about 20 years old. It struck me as unusual because I did not recognize the face. Often I see faces of friends and acquaintances in my mind. I assume this means they need an extra prayer from me. But this face was totally unfamiliar, so I decided that it probably really was my imagination alone and not a *prompting* from the Holy Spirit for prayer.

However, that evening I attended a basketball game to watch my son and cheer for his team. To my amazement, the face that

I had seen in prayer belonged to one of the players on the other team. Then I prayed, for I believed surely that boy needed special prayer. There was no possible way that I could have imagined a face that I had never seen before. The image of that boy's face had to have been given me by the Holy Spirit.

Just as we can use our imagination to plan a trip to France and enjoy it even more, we can use our imagination to meet Jesus in prayer. For example, we can imagine scenes in Jesus' life, or scenes in his parables. We can imagine ourselves in these scenes and encounter Jesus' love and wisdom directly.

Once I did a Scripture meditation on the call to follow Jesus as explained in Chapter Five of the Gospel of Matthew. I pictured myself sitting on a fence and Jesus walking up and inviting me to follow him. I asked the Holy Spirit to guide my imagination in this reflection on being called as a disciple. In my mind's eye, Jesus led me into an enclosed field of cows. I said, "I don't want to go in there. I'll get kicked and step in manure." He said, "Follow me. If you stay close I'll protect you from being kicked although you may get bumped around some. The manure won't hurt because when you get to the other side of this field you can take off your boots and leave them. You won't need them on the other side."

I believe this was vivid symbolic imagery teaching me about working with others in Christian service. Somehow I had gotten the notion that when we Christians work together there should be perfect harmony and no strife. I was ignoring the reality that human frailty means well-meaning persons sometimes hurt and even insult one another. Which I suppose is why Jesus told his disciples to forgive one another seventy-times-seven times.

At any rate, I had been hurt by a co-worker I really respected and was tempted to move on into some other kind of work. But through this imagery that unfolded in my imagination, the Lord showed me that it was his desire for me to continue to work in prayer ministry and remain immersed in the Christian community. I would grow in holiness through the difficulties in human relationships.

I have thought back on that image many times when I felt myself being "bumped around" and it has given me much encouragement. I believe the Holy Spirit took the Word of God in Matthew's gospel and made it quite personal and meaningful to me through anointing my own imagination.

Sometimes, also, the Holy Spirit places ideas or impulses to action in our minds. Sometimes He reminds us of things we have forgotten. I personally think this happens more often than we realize. We just simply are not aware that the thought came from the Holy Spirit and not us.*

Imagination is a normal faculty of human nature that the Holy Spirit can use to communicate, just as our inner self uses it to manufacture pictures and ideas (and even friends!). Even though the Holy Spirit's communication comes to us through words and images in our imaginations, it is still real in the spiritual world.

It is probably appropriate to mention here that both the power of evil and strong human emotion can also produce images and ideas in our minds. It is necessary to discern which spirit is the source of the messages our imaginations produce. Learning discernment of spirits is very important for anyone seeking to hear God interiorly.

But simply put, through paying attention, listening and reflecting prayerfully, we can learn to recognize when these words and images come to us from the Holy Spirit. Jesus said that the Holy Spirit, like the wind, blows where He will (John 3:8). If we give him access, He will sometimes speak to us through our imagination in prayer. Through symbolic imagery and anointed thoughts, He can reach into the depths of our hearts.

* Fr. Michael Scanlan's book, *What Does God Want? A Practical Guide to Making Decisions* (Franciscan University Press) is strongly recommended for discernment of God's voice.

PRAYER EXERCISE TWELVE

After becoming quiet and reading these instructions, close your eyes.

Meditation:
　　Picture God the Father. What is He wearing?
　　Is He standing or sitting?
　　What sort of look is on his face. What is He doing?
　　After you have a clear picture of him in your mind,
　　speak to him about having made you.

　　Then picture Jesus in heaven. Notice the color of his robe, the expression on his face, his hands and feet.
　　After you have *looked* at him for a while, speak to him about whatever comes to your mind.

　　Then ask the Holy Spirit to place a word, a thought or a picture in your mind, now or sometime during this day.

"Grace and Peace to you from God our Father
and the Lord Jesus Christ." (Galatians 1:3)

Chapter Thirteen

Listening through Symbols, Events and Circumstances

The Holy Spirit can use symbols and events to communicate with us. We need to pray to be able to recognize these events, which become the voice of the Shepherd for us.

In Old and New Testament times, numerous incidents are recorded where people saw certain natural or human events as signs from God revealing his will or as the hand of God providing care for his people.

To a great extent, our scientific culture, which insists on a natural explanation for every happening, has distracted us from recognizing the hand of God in explainable natural events. We are led to believe that if an event has a natural explanation, then God had nothing to do with it. This is a great sad error. By believing this, we have lost sight of the magnificence of the providence and power of God and of his purposeful intervention in human affairs — even our own personal affairs.

I believe that God often sends us manifestations of his love and concern through happenings that may have a natural explanation but also have a supernatural impetus behind them — the hand of God. If we have eyes to see, we will receive great blessings from recognizing these events.

One such event that happened to me involved the appearance in my front yard of a mysterious rare bird. It was a wonderful, kind, compassionate action of the Lord in my life. I and all my family recognized it as a gift from God, because, while natural, it was very unusual.

Our older son, Matt, was away for his third year of college and our younger son, Chris, had recently left home to join him at the same college for his freshman year. Mark and I were experiencing the loneliness of the empty nest. Truly, we were very, very sad. Our years of daily family intimacy with children around the dinner table and involvement in their daily lives had come to an end. Both our sons were now away seeking their own destinies. It was very right and very good. And while we were proud, in a certain way we were also sad.

I went through a kind of grieving process. During this time, the Holy Spirit consoled me and spoke to me by sending a lost, tame, rare bird. I realize that it sounds outrageous to suggest that God would send a bird to help fill an *empty nest*, but I can only say that this did really happen.

I noticed this beautiful red, orange and brown bird a few mornings just outside my front door, pecking around for food. A friend suggested putting out bird seed, and she brought some over. As she threw the seed toward the bird, she noticed with delight that the bird came very close to her, clearly not afraid of people. A few mornings later I decided to try to feed him out of my hand. He came and ate! Next I sat down on the curb and invited him to hop into my lap to eat. He did.

We began a daily morning ritual. I would come out and sit down with the bird with the seed in my hand, and He would hop into my lap and eat from my hand. While this was going on, I would experience in my *gut* a deep satisfying feeling quite similar to the feeling I had when I fed my sons as infants. I suppose you could call it a mother's fulfillment through nurturing.

Mark and I made phone inquiries and looked in the classified ads for lost birds, but found no owner. This bird remained voluntarily in our yard for more than a year. During that time I was not only consoled by this extraordinary experience, which I knew was somehow supernaturally initiated and sustained, but I also was instructed in the art of Christian nurturing. I have applied the lessons I learned to my work of teaching spirituality and doing prayer ministry. In fact, I often prayerfully reflected on nurturing others as I fed the bird, recognizing that it was a grace being given me.

The biggest lesson I learned was that of nurturing without controlling. The bird would come into my lap and eat, but he would never allow me to grab or hold him. He trusted me enough to jump on my lap, but would flee if I made any move toward his body other than extending my hand with the seed. And my deepest instincts told me it would destroy the gift should I ever try to capture and cage this fellow. He liked to be close so long as he was free.

At night the bird had a second ritual. As dusk approached, he would hop up on one certain branch of a tree beside my house and sit there until sunrise. The branch where he sat at night was directly beside the seat where I pray each day — separated of course by the wall of my house. At sunrise, he would hop down and chirp with the other birds around the yard. I could recognize his chirp as I lay in bed, and it always seemed that he was rejoicing in another new day.

I called him Sweetie. Mark and I wondered what kind of bird he was. He had magnificent colors, but we didn't recognize the markings. I looked through several North American bird books but could not find a bird that looked like him. Then one day Mark called from his office. "Carol, you're not going to believe this, but there is a picture of Sweetie in the hallway just outside my office door. He's called a Chinese Pheasant." An Audubon painting of the bird had been in the hall just outside Mark's office door for more than 20 years, but he had never paid close attention until that day when something (probably the Holy Spirit) prompted him to look closely at it.

Sweetie remained in our yard for more than a year, pecking around by day and sleeping on the same branch each night, just outside the window of the room where I pray. Then one day he just disappeared. I suspected that a cat I occasionally had seen stalking in the yard finally frightened Sweetie away. I knew that God had sent the bird, so I felt I should just accept that it was God's timing for him to move on and to leave his *destiny* in the Lord's hands.

This bird did reappear once more about a year later. It was the day Mark's father died. We had stayed up most of the night watching and praying with Dad. He went with the angels about four a.m. By the time we returned to our house, the sun was rising. We looked out into our back yard and, to our utter amazement, there was Sweetie! This time he stayed only a couple of weeks, and then left for good. The timing of this appearance, however, served to reaffirm to us that it was no coincidence that this bird had appeared in our yard.

The good Lord had sent him for a reason with a message. He consoled me in a funny way and showed me something about loving and letting go. I thank God for this gift, for lovingly speaking to me through a bird.

PRAYER EXERCISE THIRTEEN

Meditation:

Take a walk alone outside of your home. Keeping silence and a listening frame of mind, look for some object which may be a symbol for the Holy Spirit to speak to you about the goodness of God.

Once you have determined which object is bringing you this symbolic message, ask the Lord to reveal to your heart anything specific He may want to say to you through it.

"For creation waits with eager expectation for the revelation of the children of God." (Romans 8:19)

Chapter Fourteen

Listening Through the Words
of Another Person

Occasionally, a friend or family member will say something strong to me with such conviction that I ask myself, "Is the Lord trying to tell me something by inspiring this person with a message from the Holy Spirit?" My husband in particular seems to bring me such messages. Sometimes I appreciate them; sometimes, I don't! He might say, for example, "Carol, you need to stop worrying so much about that," or, "Have you spoken with so and so lately?" Often these words have proven to be true guidance for my good.

Now I don't believe that everything Mark says is directly from the Holy Spirit. Some things definitely are not! But I have found over our years of marriage and mutual loving concern, that sometimes the Holy Spirit catches my attention through his words.

Others not so close to us, or even strangers for that matter, can be instruments of the Lord speaking to us. Once many years ago when I was riding on a train, the conductor stopped by my seat, placed his hands on my head and said, "The Lord wants to give you the gift of knowledge." I was embarrassed at the time, hoping no one else on the train noticed such a strange occurrence. But reflecting later, I realized that the Holy Spirit wanted me to know God had a plan for me to teach spiritual things to others. Because I was a lay woman, not a nun or a priest, I needed some extra encouragement to believe in this call.

Recently we had a problem in my family. While this particular crisis did not affect me directly, it caused much sorrow and anxiety for my brother, whom I love very much. I found myself not only praying for him but also worrying for him, almost to the point of making myself sick.

One morning while in prayer about this, I picked up a Bible and began to open it. A holy card fell out which had a picture of a little bird standing under a mushroom plant. Water was dripping from the mushroom cap into the mouth of the bird. The words on the card said, "All is in the providence of God." A friend had sent me this card more than a year before. I had stuck it in the pages of this particular Bible, which I hadn't picked up for a while.

Now, at this particular moment of anxiety, the Holy Spirit was speaking through the card which *accidentally* fell in my lap. I thought to myself, "Well, even my brother's problem could be in the providence of God for some good reason." Then I forgot about it until the next day when I was sitting in front of the Blessed Sacrament in prayer. I was just sitting silently thinking of nothing in particular when the image of that mushroom flashed vividly back into my mind. Because I wasn't thinking of my brother's difficulty at that particular moment, I felt confident that the Holy Spirit, not the power of suggestion, had placed that image in my mind. So then I realized that the Lord was telling me to trust that He was at work for good through my brother's circumstances. I needed to stop worrying and start trusting!

Later in the day I had a confirmation of this message through the words of another person. I happened to be at a talk given by a holy priest with many charismatic gifts. I asked him afterward to pray for my brother. He took my hands and said, "The first thing that comes to my mind is that you are not to worry but to trust that your brother is in the Lord's hands and give thanks in prayer that God's providence is working."

The Lord was using another to reach me because he knew it was so difficult for me to accept that I should stop worrying. The Holy Spirit was speaking, trying to help me.

PRAYER EXERCISE FOURTEEN

Recall five significant people who have touched your life. Possibly a parent, a brother or sister, a teacher, a spouse or a friend. Or possibly, someone else. Maybe even someone you didn't know that well personally. List them below:

1) _____

2) _____

3) _____

4) _____

5) _____

Prayerfully think back to times with each person. Try to recognize whether there might have been a time when the Lord was helping you by inspiring their words or actions.

*"We should consider how to rouse one another to
love and good works." (Hebrews 10:24)*

Chapter Fifteen

Receptivity in Listening

E ven after one has recognized the voice of the Holy Spirit speaking, be it through scripture, inner thoughts, other symbols or other people, there is another important element: receptivity. Jesus talks about being receptive in a parable:

"A sower went out to sow. And as he sowed, some seeds fell along the path, and the birds came and devoured them. Other seeds fell on rocky ground, where they had not much soil, and immediately they sprang up, since they had no depth of soil, but when the sun rose they were scorched; and since they had no root they withered away. Other seeds fell upon thorns, and the thorns grew up and choked them. Other seeds fell on good soil and brought forth grain, some a hundred-fold, some sixty, some thirty." (Matthew 13:3-8)

The parable of the sower tells us that the word of God lands inside our hearts with varying degrees of effectiveness. Some gets carried away by the evil one, some gets lost in our worldly cares, some is rejected by the part of us that is hard-hearted, but some lands in our deepest selves where it connects with the power of the Holy Spirit and brings forth new life.

Where is our good soil? Why doesn't all the seed find its way there? I am sure it has to do with our human, psychological complexity. We build walls to defend our inner selves. Sometimes trapped in self-defense, we resist hearing God's life-giving word.

It is possible to hear and not to listen. It is also possible to hear, to listen and to then refuse to accept the message. We habitually do this with other people for legitimate reasons: when we do not think they are correct in what they are saying; when we know that it will be bad of us to entertain what they are saying, as in gossip; or when we simply recognize that what they are saying is of no concern to us.

However, if God is speaking, it is another story! Jesus told those who believed and listened to him, "Blessed are your eyes, because they see, and your ears, because they hear. Amen, I say to you, many prophets and righteous people longed to see what you see but did not see it, and to hear what you hear but did not hear it." (Matthew 13:1-17)

A friend once told me this story: She was home one holiday season packing some old clothes in a box to take to a homeless shelter. It was a cold winter and the clothes she was discarding were warm. As she prepared to leave her house to drive to the shelter, she heard an inner voice say, "Don't go!" She believed it was the Holy Spirit prompting her but couldn't believe what He was saying. She was confused. She couldn't imagine why the Lord would not want her to give these clothes to some poor, cold person. But she heeded this voice and did not go to deliver the clothes.

A few moments later, there came a knock on her door. A desperate looking young woman was there. She told my friend that she was despondent and no longer wanted to live. She was preparing to take her own life when she had the idea that she should give herself one more chance to find hope by going to speak with my friend who she knew was a strong Christian woman. So she came over and knocked on my friend's door!

Fortunately, in that case, two people were receptive to the voice of the Holy Spirit!

There is one more important principle of receptivity. We must wait for the Holy Spirit to speak according to *God's timing*. We cannot call forth words, as if by magic, when we want to hear them. God is the ruler of time and so his timing must necessarily be perfect. We are the ones who get anxious. We must simply go to God in prayer, to love and honor him, and trust that He will speak to us in his timing, not our own.

We cannot determine when the Holy Spirit should speak to

us any more than we can make the sun rise in the morning. God takes the initiative through the Holy Spirit. He alone causes his word to dawn in our hearts in answer to our prayer, just as He alone makes the light of the morning sky.

By waking up early, waiting and watching, we can share in the beauty of the morning dawn. We do so, expecting the sunrise to happen. In the same way, we take steps in prayer to open ourselves to the Lord. Then we wait for the dawning of his word.

One morning not long ago I awakened early to pray and enjoy some peace and quiet with the Lord. It was a Sunday morning and I was curled up comfortably on a sofa with my Bible, enjoying the early morning through my window. But suddenly I heard an insistent voice within my soul say, "Get up and go to the eight a.m. Mass." It was unusual because Mark and I have rarely gone to that Mass. We really enjoy making Sunday leisurely by going to one of the later masses.

But in this case, I was pretty sure that the Holy Spirit was speaking so I reluctantly got dressed and hurried to church alone. As it turned out, the priest saying that Mass, one who had been in our parish for a number of years, was saying his very last Sunday Mass because he was going to die two weeks later of cancer. I could see it was an effort for him to get through the service, but of course, like everyone else, did not realize how near was his departure from this world.

Because of the unusual prompting I had received, I decided to speak to him afterward. I waited in the back of the church and, as he came out the door, I said hello and asked about his health. He invited me into the rectory for a cup of coffee.

Our conversation led into a discussion about death and dying. I was able to share with him a very moving experience I had years before with another priest who had courageously faced death from cancer and moved triumphantly into eternity. I sensed my story was encouraging to this wonderful priest who was suffering so. At the end of our conversation, we had some prayer time together and I went home.

That very night the priest went into sudden severe distress and was admitted to the hospital. I never saw him again. But I believe the Lord had spoken to me and sent me to him with a particular message of encouragement that he needed on his walk toward eternity. His close friends tell me he died peacefully, looking forward to meeting the Lord. I felt so blessed to have been a part of God's gentle process of preparing this loving priest for his return home.

For me this experience resulted from the voice of the Lord breaking into my morning prayer and, fortunately, on that day I was receptive.

PRAYER EXERCISE FIFTEEN

Wake up very early one morning. Go outside with a chair and watch and wait for the sunrise. Listen to the Holy Spirit in your heart while it is still dark. Listen in your heart when the sun first appears in the sky. Listen in your heart as the sun majestically reaches its place in the morning sky.

Conclude with these words:

Blessed be the name of God forever and ever,
for wisdom and power are his.
He causes the changes of the times and seasons,
makes kings and unmakes them.
He gives wisdom to the wise and knowledge to
those who understand.
He reveals deep and hidden things,
and knows what is in the darkness,
for the light dwells with him.

(Daniel 2:20-22)

"Blessed be the name of God." (Daniel 2:20)

Chapter Sixteen

Simply Listening

There is a fascinating Bible story in which Jesus' disciples try to keep children away from him, presumably because they thought these small ones would only tire him out and interfere with his mission. Jesus, however, calls the children to him and says the most startling thing: "Let the children come to me and do not prevent them; for the kingdom of God belongs to such as these. Amen, I say to you, whoever does not accept the kingdom of God like a child will not enter it." (Luke 18:16-17)

At another time, complimenting his disciples on obediently following his command to go proclaim the kingdom of God, Jesus said: "I give you praise, Father, Lord of heaven and earth for what you have hidden from the wise and the learned you have revealed to the childlike. Yes, such has been your will." (Luke 10:21)

Now I don't know about you but growing up in my neighborhood I was never complimented for being childlike. Rather, I learned to put on the appearance of competence, sophistication and intelligence so that I could survive the pressures to be successful and socially acceptable. Inside was a child longing for appreciation and respect, but she was buried beneath the outer shell. And as the years went by, I found myself identifying more and more with this outer shell. I would say it even robbed me of some of the joy of my early marriage years where my learned sophistication was an obstacle to emotional intimacy with my husband.

But the place where sophistication proved most inappropriate was in my walk with the Lord, once I had said "yes" to him. I did not know how to trust him with childlike simplicity because I had unlearned *being simple* as part of growing up. I did not know how to approach God with the awe and wonder of a child. I had a lot to learn, or rather, to unlearn.

I believe that it is a major challenge of the Holy Spirit to teach us simplicity of heart. If we doubt that God wants this, we can look carefully at all the main characters in the Gospels. They were simple people — fishermen, tax collectors and even prostitutes. Weak maybe, but simple, and willing to trust and learn. When Peter told Jesus that he understood that Jesus was the Messiah, the son of the living God, Jesus replied, "Blessed are you, Simon, son of Jonah. For flesh and blood has not revealed this to you, but my heavenly Father." (Matthew 16:17) In other words, "You, Peter, did not figure this out through your own intelligence; rather, it was revealed to you by God."

On the other hand, Jesus regarded the sophisticated ones, the Pharisees who were learned and scrupulously legalistic in their teaching about religion, as the bad guys. He told them, "Woe to you, scholars of the law! You have taken away the key of knowledge. You yourselves did not enter and you stopped those trying to enter." (Luke 11:52) It seems that Jesus was trying to tell these educated and highly respected men that their knowledge could not save them from the wrath of God. Indeed, their use of that knowledge only insulated their hearts from the truth of their frailty before God. The fortunate ones, rather, were those who in their simplicity turned to God and asked for his help.

A friend told me a story once that illustrated this principle very clearly. It is the story of a brilliant man who was asked to present a paper on the Twenty-third Psalm at a conference on spirituality. The man was very inspired by the invitation and studiously prepared a presentation in which he carefully uncovered the deep meanings of the psalm. His presentation was applauded loudly.

But while this speaker was returning to his seat from the

podium, a simple old man, who happened to be in the conference hall refilling the coffee urn, spontaneously approached the stage. He went to the microphone and began to recite the Twenty-third Psalm very slowly and with all the love in his heart pouring out. The audience was moved to tears by the man's words. After completing the psalm, "And I shall dwell in the house of the Lord for years to come," the old man returned to the back of the room.

The original presenter then returned to the microphone and said: "Dear friends, as you could tell from my presentation, I know the Twenty-third Psalm. But this man who has just spoken — he knows the Shepherd!"

It takes a childlike person to know the Shepherd and his voice. It is only when we put aside our worldly sophistication that we can truly hear the voice of God through the power of the Holy Spirit. The Spirit himself will show us how to listen with childlike simplicity as we begin to follow his lead.

PRAYER EXERCISE SIXTEEN

Sing this children's song to yourself, either out loud or in your mind:

> Jesus loves me, this I know,
> for the Bible tells me so.
> Little ones to him belong.
> They are weak but He is strong.
> Yes, Jesus loves me.
> Yes, Jesus loves me.
> Yes, Jesus loves me.
> The Bible tells me so.

Next, imagine Jesus seated on a bench watching children play at your neighborhood playground. You walk toward him from outside the playground area. You call to him, "Lord, may I come sit on the bench and speak with you?"

He answers...

"For the kingdom of God belongs to such as these." (Luke 18:16)

Chapter Seventeen

Developing the Habit of Listening

In my kitchen next to the faucet in the sink is a sprayer hose for rinsing the dishes. Do you know I hardly ever use that hose? It is in my line of vision daily, but I hardly ever think to pick it up and use it, even though it would make rinsing the dishes a cleaner and easier job.

Why? Because I am a creature of habit. Before I moved into my present house almost thirty years ago, I never had a sink sprayer. I got used to rinsing the dishes without one. And I have never changed my style of rinsing dishes in the nearly thirty years I've had a sprayer daily staring me in the face.

In fact, it was only a few years ago that I even noticed the sprayer and thought about the amazing fact that for so many years I had never used it. But what is more unbelievable to me, since this amazing discovery I have still not developed the habit of using the sprayer. Habit is difficult to change.

This analogy, unfortunately, is a good image of our use of God's gift of the Holy Spirit. He is not only in front of us, but within us! Yet we try in many ways to live the Christian life without his help and guidance. We are used to our own ways.

He will help us understand what is difficult to understand. He will help us to do what is difficult or even humanly impossible when it is God's will for us. He will bring us into a beautiful, intimate friendship with God our Father and Jesus our Lord.

But the habit of relying on our own thoughts and ideas is strong in us. We hesitate to listen to the Holy Spirit. We forget to ask for his help. We sometimes make things complicated that are really very simple. Meanwhile, the Holy Spirit is waiting for us to turn to him and listen.

To return to a beginning point of this book, our challenge of living Christian discipleship is magnified by the environment of the 21st century technological society in which we live. We certainly can use all the help we can get. The Holy Spirit is a helper. Just as the daily task of rinsing dishes could become easier for me if I would simply pick up the sink sprayer, meeting the challenges of Christian discipleship would become easier for us if we simply start to listen to the Holy Spirit.

So, let us begin!

 So, let us begin!

PRAYER EXERCISE SEVENTEEN

Recollect yourself. Speak to the Holy Spirit about helping you to develop a better prayer life, with regular listening to him included.

Some things to consider:

1. What place in my home can I make a permanent *Prayer Corner* for myself? (You can arrange a Bible, pictures, prayer books nearby.)

2. What time of day can I schedule regularly into my planning for quiet time with the Lord? How can I include time for *listening* in addition to my current prayer practices?

3. How will I use Scripture in my prayer time? (Go methodically through one of the Gospels; or follow a published daily Scripture meditation book; or follow the lectionary readings; or randomly open Scripture when sitting down to pray.)

4. Are there some other people around experienced in prayer to talk with me about my prayer experiences — especially when I think the Holy Spirit might be *talking* to me?

5. How could I effectively use a journal in my personal prayer life? Should I write in it every day, or just when I think the Lord has spoken with me? Do I want to write meaningful Scripture passages in my journal?

Listening Prayer and the Sacramental Life

Some Catholics have asked the question, "How does the style of listening prayer described in this book relate to my regular practice of our Catholic faith? My spirituality is basically sacramental."

Simply put, listening to God in personal prayer intertwines with the sacramental life and deepens our reception of the graces He gives us. At Mass, the Liturgy of the Word is all about listening to God's *word* to us. Then we are given the gift of Jesus in the Eucharist. We eat his Body and drink his Blood, bringing a continual nourishing of his life within us. In the few moments following reception of communion we can listen for his voice, bringing his words to our thoughts. Our focus and faith are strengthened, as well as our souls.

Also, we have the privilege of visiting our Eucharistic Lord by making a church visit. When we spend time in silent adoration before the Blessed Sacrament Jesus can speak to our hearts, as we are receptive to hearing Him. Some people in fact find they are most receptive to inspirations from the Holy Spirit when they are alone in church in the silent presence of the Eucharist.

In the sacrament of Reconciliation, we can hear Jesus' words through the healing of total forgiveness and the counsel of the priest as we attune ourselves to the Holy Spirit speaking through him. We may also receive an inspiration as we do our penance with an open heart.

So, why do we need to take time with personal prayer when we have the sacraments? The answer is given in the *Catechism of the Catholic Church*: "whereas the sacraments are efficacious signs of grace by which divine life is dispensed to us" (1131)... "we are prepared for the sacraments by the Word of God and the faith which welcomes that word in well-disposed hearts" (1133). We enter into this preparation process by personal prayer, which disposes us to open our hearts to all God's gifts.

Dear Lord, grant to us listening ears and a listening heart!

Suggestions for Use
in
Personal Prayer
and Small Groups

The goal of the book *The Sound of His Voice* is to help people to draw closer to Jesus in personal prayer. This happens partly when a person becomes more aware of the inspirations of the Holy Spirit within him or her. Growing in this awareness is a key theme in the book.

Through this book and its suggested prayer exercises, you may well discover a new dimension to personal prayer that will really enrich your life. It will be well worth the amount of time you set aside at home to do the exercises.

If, in addition, you are participating in a small group you will find this effort, and the sharing of your thoughts, more beneficial to both you and the group. Make every effort to spend the time at home in quiet prior to the meeting!

PRAYING WITH *THE SOUND OF HIS VOICE*

■ Find 15-30 minutes in which you can be quiet and alone for each assigned chapter.

■ Get comfortable. Spend a few minutes quieting yourself possibly repeating a few familiar prayers.

■ Pray the following from Psalm 43: 1-3
As a deer longs for running waters,
so my soul longs for you, O God.
A thirst is my soul for God, the living God.
When shall I go and behold the face of God?

■ Read the assigned chapter in the book. Note any questions or related concerns you might want to bring to the group.

■ Do the meditation which follows the chapter.

■ In a notebook or journal, write a description of what happened when you did the suggested meditation. You could add any thoughts or reflections relating to God that come to mind as you are writing your description.

■ Complete the prayer time with a prayer of your choosing.

One possible closing prayer:

Psalm 103: 1-4 (paraphrased)
Bless the Lord, O my soul;
and all my being bless his holy name.
Bless the Lord, O my soul and forget not all his benefits.
He pardons all our sins He heals all our ills.
He redeems our life from destruction.
He crowns us with kindness and compassion.

Thank you, Lord for being close to me. Amen.

GENERAL FORMAT FOR GROUP MEETINGS
USING *THE SOUND OF HIS VOICE*

(This is a suggested general format and may be adapted to the situation of a particular group)

■ Greeting by facilitator and opening prayer.

■ One to three minutes of group silence, allowing each person to recollect self and reflect on the presence of the Lord. (Some groups play music quietly in the background during this time.)

■ Synopsis by the facilitator of the material in the assigned chapter (for 2-3 minutes).

■ Comments by others in the group about the material in the chapter.

■ Sharing by each group member on the experience of the chapter meditation. This is the "heart" of the group meeting.*

Important Note: There is no "right" or "wrong" way to experience these mediations. Where one's heart and the Holy Spirit together take a person in his or her quiet time is always good. People will often report vastly different experiences because of the uniqueness of each person. Listening to how another in the group related with God in the meditation is often enriching to all.

■ Synopsis by the facilitator (or other designated person) of next assigned chapter if more than one was assigned, followed by comments others might want to make.

■ Sharing by group members on the experience of the meditation (Repeat this process for each assigned chapter).

■ Facilitator mentions the assigned chapter or chapters for the next meeting.

■ Closing prayer.

GUIDELINES FOR PRAYER GROUP PARTICIPANTS
USING *THE SOUND OF HIS VOICE*

■ This is a program which depends on sharing by participants at the small group meetings. You will be surprised how much something that you share may help another.

■ It is important to take time to do the assigned personal prayer exercises at home. This provides the basis for the small group time.

■ Everyone needs to be given an opportunity to share. Sometimes you may not want to share and that is okay.

■ There is an "equal time" rule. No one person should dominate the group's time with lengthy sharing, even if unintentional. It is the facilitator's role to ask people to observe this rule should someone get "carried away."

■ The sharing sessions are to be focused on the prayer exercises done at home, NOT personal problems, theological opinions, gossip or promotion of a cause - even a worthy one.

■ It is not appropriate to give advice to someone during the group session. If a person seeks advice from you, speak to one another after the session concludes.

■ This is not a time for teaching or lecturing, unless the facilitator may be teaching a principle of prayer related to the subject matter at hand.

■ Everyone's experience with the prayer exercises is valid. There is no right or wrong answer, just prayer experiences with the Lord.

■ A promise of CONFIDENTIALITY is asked and expected of each group member, giving one another freedom to share sensitive feelings or personal information relevant to a prayer experience, if desired.

■ It is important to give support and cooperation to the group facilitator who is charged with the responsibility of seeing that these group guidelines are followed.

Introducing...

Everyday Principles for Listening to God

Prayer Program

Introduction

OUR FIAT is a small group program designed to help people draw close to God in a personal relationship through scriptural meditation and prayerful listening to the Holy Spirit. It combines daily personal prayer with weekly small group sharing and is easy to use in both small individual groups and as a general parish format.

OUR FIAT offers a way for ordinary people to answer Jesus' calls of "Follow me," and "Abide in me." It teaches one to discern the Holy Spirit's voice. It encourages prayer becoming a two-way communication where one can experience God's love and presence more deeply. It is based on praying with the scriptures. It is appropriate for people from all walks of life.

OUR FIAT helps people develop the habit of daily prayer. Prayer exercises that are provided encourage faith-filled dialogue with God. Group sharing of prayer experiences helps participants to further reflect on how God manifests himself in their personal prayer experiences.

THE OUR FIAT PROGRAM

OUR FIAT is a spiritual life program. It provides a step-by-step sequence of ongoing prayer exercises for group members to do individually at home. Weekly, group members meet together to share the experiences and describe the graces received through personal prayer. People grow in understanding of how God works in their lives by listening to one another's sharing.

The prayer exercises themselves revolve around the practice of *lectio divina* - that is - meditating on the scriptures. In a simple way they incorporate the prayer forms of The Spiritual Exercises of St. Ignatius: noticing which line in a scripture passage seems to stand out; imaginatively dialoguing with Jesus as presented in the scriptures; and using imagination - placing oneself in scripture scenes.

The overall program provides a four-step sequence of exercises which are available as separate books. The first step is an introductory set of exercises and can be presented to a large group. The remaining steps are taken in sequence by interested small faith sharing groups at a time and place to be determined by each continuing group. Participants can begin with the introductory exercises and then continue with as many of the steps as they desire. Each step in the program is valuable in itself.

THE PURPOSE OF THE *OUR FIAT* PROGRAM AND ITS BENEFITS

The purpose of the program is to provide a format to facilitate people's drawing closer to God through personal prayer leading to a greater awareness of God's loving action in their lives. The following are some of the benefits of participating in the program:

■ Learning to dialogue in a fruitful and meaningful way with the risen Lord. Another way of saying this is growing into an intimate personal relationship with God who created each person for a specific purpose.

■ Entering into a special type of friendship with other members in a small group. The saints and the tradition of our Church would call this a spiritual friendship. Spiritual friends offer support, encouragement and helpful insights in one's relationship to God. A unique bond exists between such friends.

■ Answering a particular call of Pope Benedict XVI to draw close to the Lord and live in his will through *lectio divina*. Pope Benedict XVI has said that he believes this practice will lead the Church into a "new springtime."

■ Coming spiritually alive in a new way. Many who have participated in this program find that other activities and relationships in life take on a new, more vivid hue, under the shining light of the Holy Spirit's inspiration.

■ Learning to yield to the grace of God, thereby allowing that grace to accomplish things within a person's life that could never be accomplished by willpower or one's own personal strength.

HOW *OUR FIAT* MAY BE USED

■ As a general parish program.

■ By existing small faith communities looking for new material.

■ By those interested in forming a small faith-sharing group.

■ For people that have completed the RCIA program and who want to improve their spiritual life.

An Outline of the Four Steps of the *OUR FIAT* Program

Step One: *THE SOUND OF HIS VOICE*

The Sound of His Voice is an introduction to prayer exercises that allows participants, within a six-week session, to determine if this program is right for them.

Participants learn the process and principles of listening to the Holy Spirit within, the sound of Jesus' voice. We may want to say "yes" to God, as Mary did. But in order to know what God wants of us to be able to say "yes," we need to understand how to listen to what He is saying in the depths of our hearts.

Step Two:
FOUNDATIONS OF PERSONAL PRAYER

Participating in the *Foundations of Personal Prayer* exercises in this step allows the individual to develop a deeper personal relationship with the Holy Trinity. There are segments on relating to God the Father, Jesus and the Holy Spirit. There is an additional section on relating in prayer to the Blessed Virgin Mary. The intended fruits of this step are growth in confidence of God's loving presence in one's life, increased personal faith and developing the habit of daily prayer.

Step Three: *LIVING STONES*

Often someone who has completed *Foundations of Personal Prayer* and developed a better recognition of what the Holy Spirit may be saying in their own heart, develops the desire to follow Jesus in a more deliberate commitment. It is important to learn how to better cooperate with the graces given to actually do what God is asking. The exercises in *Living Stones* help people open their hearts to the Holy Spirit's transforming power and reflect upon their personal call to selfless Christian service. There is encouragement to see one's life in the context of God's plan.

Step Four: *WALLS AND BRIDGES*

Practically everyone has been formed by some life experiences that inhibit them from freely embracing all that God wants for them. Habits and attitudes developed earlier in life can become obstacles to discipleship. The prayer exercises in *Walls and Bridges* focus upon allowing the Holy Spirit to transform hearts through interior healing. Such healing allows people to more fully know God's love and more freely answer his call.

WHY THE PROGRAM IS NAMED *OUR FIAT*

The program encourages imitation of the Blessed Virgin Mary, who, when invited to become the mother of Jesus through the power of the Holy Spirit, responded, "Let it be done to me," (In Latin: "Fiat"). Participants are encouraged to add their own personal "fiat" to that of Mary and ask her prayerful intercession for needed graces. Hence, the name, "OUR FIAT."

"Our Fiat" means our yes to God. When we, the baptized, say "yes" to God, and to his purpose for our life, we are overshadowed by the same Spirit of God who formed Jesus in Mary's womb. As we take steps to cooperate with the Spirit's work within us, the spirit of Jesus is formed in our hearts. We become better witnesses in our time and circumstances.

Scripture tells us that in her desire to live in the will of God, Mary pondered prayerfully the events in her life. Participants in this program are encouraged to do the same, spending time in prayerful listening and reflection in addition to participation in the sacramental life of the Church.

WHY THIS PROGRAM IS NEEDED NOW

The tradition of the Church has always emphasized the importance of prayer along with Christian action yet many people today do not know how to develop a good personal prayer life. In addition, the secular humanist mind-set of today's culture discourages people from taking time for prayer.

St. John of the Cross has said that the two most important decisions anyone can make in their life are: 1) To turn one's life over to Christ; and 2) To make a commitment to personal prayer. This program brings encouragement to daily turn one's life over to Christ and to pray.

What Some Others Have

This prayer program has proved highly beneficial to the prayer life and faith life of those who have experienced it. I am happy to endorse the program and encourage as many Christians as possible to deepen their own prayer and faith life by involvement in this program.

W. Thomas Larkin
Bishop Emeritus,
Diocese of St. Petersburg

The greatest experience in Christian life is to have a personal relationship with Jesus, and the heart of that relationship is the give and take communication that we know as prayer. This program teaches practical ways of talking and, especially, listening to God. I highly recommend it.

Fr. Bill McCarthy, MSA
Author, teacher and Director of
My Father's House Retreat Center

Under the warmth of the spiritual motherhood of Mary, the OUR FIAT program brings out the deep spiritual life of men and women as they move in the 'world,' growing in the grace and image of Jesus. This program offers to our lives the life of Jesus in a very practical manner, arranging, step-by-step, points of thought for reflection and prayer. Here in meditation is a scheduled, systematic presentation of spirituality. It allows us to set the meaning of the Gospel in our lives. The Word takes root. Since its inception in my parish in 2002, its value to those living the Gospel has been treasured with great enthusiasm and joy. It has inspired me, the participants and the parish. The Word yields a hundred-fold.

Fr. Jules Brunet
Our Lady of Prompt Succor Parish
Diocese of Baton Rouge, Louisiana

Said About the Program

The letters in the word F-I-A-T have special meaning to me. They describe what this program does: Fosters Interior Awakening and Transformation.

Bob H.

In my busy life, I had so many distractions from keeping me still. I personally needed an organized prayer program to develop my habit of sitting still. Since there are no instant habits, I started practicing the discipline of praying with the OUR FIAT scriptures each morning and waiting to hear from the Lord. Now it is a regular part of every day. I look forward to my quiet time and to what the Lord wants to tell me.

Connie S.

I was raised Catholic, went to Catholic schools and college and have practiced my faith all of my life. But I never found the depth of meaning and life-giving power of personal prayer until I participated in this program.

Mark M.

When I started OUR FIAT I had no idea what was in store for me, except that I was hungry to learn about this man, Jesus. He has placed beautiful windows in my soul where his light enters in. God has helped me see myself. He has healed me, helped me mend fences from past squabbles and hurts. His hand is always there to lead me with his tender touch.

Margie D.

I am a wife and mother and a cancer survivor. Because of my prayer life which has developed through participation in the OUR FIAT program, I have been changed. The program proved very valuable in facing the challenge of cancer and learning to be the best wife and mother that I can be. Reading the scriptures, praying, doing the exercises, taking the time to journal and ultimately sharing with the group on a weekly basis brought me the courage and support I needed through the difficulties that I have faced.

Cathy S.

The prayer exercises in the OUR FIAT program were developed by participants in a network of small prayer and faith-sharing groups called Mantle of Mary. This network developed through interaction of lay Catholics interested in growing in the spiritual life through prayer with scripture, asking the intercession of the Blessed Virgin Mary. Much of the composition of the exercises was done by Carol Marquardt, the author of *The Sound Of His Voice.*

Use of the prayer exercises spread spontaneously around the Diocese of St. Petersburg, Florida and into Arkansas, Idaho, Louisiana, Mexico and Peru. Eventually the group leaders sought ecclesial approbation that the program might be made available in other places with official Church sanction. In May of 2006 the program received the blessing of the Bishop of St. Petersburg, Most Reverend Robert N. Lynch. It received the Nihil Obstat after review by Fr. David Toups, S.T.D. in September 2006.

The team that has prepared the materials for use by others includes:

Delia Colson	Gabriella Mullins
Mark Fanders	Sr. Marjorie Quin, CSJ
Cathy Hodge	Fr. Gilberto Quintero, OFM
Gilma Huie	Helen Ross
Roberto Huie	Connie Schudmak
Sr. Kathleen Luger, OSC	Jeff Signorini
Carol Marquardt	Cathy Suglia
Dan Morrison	Bernadine Wright

To begin the *OUR FIAT* program in your parish or small group or for more information please contact us... 877-OUR-FIAT or 727-446-6515

About the Author

Carol Marquardt, M.A. has spent many years working in lay ministry in the Catholic Diocese of St. Petersburg, Florida. Prior to establishing the Mantle of Mary Association - which led to the development of the OUR FIAT program - Carol served as an adult education director, catechumenate director, retreat house director and charismatic prayer group leader. She has worked in inner healing ministry and spiritual direction,  and has led pilgrimages to Marian shrines such as Medjugorje, Lourdes and Guadelupe, as well as to Rome and Assisi; She has also participated in evangelization missions to Eastern Europe with Renewal Ministries of Ann Arbor, Michigan.

Developing the Mantle of Mary prayer network and the *OUR FIAT Prayer Program* has been Carol's primary work for the last ten years. Beginning with one small group seeking a deeper spiritual life, she wrote a series of prayer exercises to guide those interested in spending quiet, quality time alone in silence for personal prayer. Over time these evolved into the *OUR FIAT Prayer Program*. As other groups formed, and existing groups sought more prayer materials, she developed what is now a three-year program based on daily individual prayer exercises and weekly group meetings to support one another. *The Sound of His Voice* was written to introduce the concept of listening to the Holy Spirit, the basis of the *OUR FIAT* program.

A graduate of Duke University, Carol holds Masters Degrees in Education (University of Illinois) and Pastoral Ministry (St. Thomas University, Miami).

Teacher and author Father Bill McCarthy, MSA says: "Carol's writings reflect not only a personal experience that she has with the Lord, but a practical, pastoral way to teach others to do so. I highly recommend her books."

131

Prayer Program

our fiat

Listening and Responding to God

The Sound of His Voice
The Introduction to the Series

This first book allows participants to experience the program in a short six-week session. Individuals can quickly determine if this program is right for them. Group members learn the process and principles of listening to the sound of Jesus' voice.

Foundations of Personal Prayer
Exercise Book One

This 30-week session allows participants to develop a deeper personal relationship with the Holy Trinity and friendship with Mary resulting in a greater prayer and faith life.

Living Stones
Exercise Book Two

During this 25-week session participants become more attentive and open to God's grace working in their individual hearts and lives that all may live out their special calling.

Walls and Bridges
Exercise Book Three

This 20-week session will allow participants to experience a deeper opening of their hearts in surrender to God's love and healing touch.

MANTLE PUBLISHING
1-877-OUR-FIAT • WWW.OURFIAT.ORG